Praise for Shoes ot a Servant ~

Diane Benscoter's epic journey in wearing the *Shoes of a Servant* reveals a mind lost to mind-controlling manipulators in a powerful cult, and then not only found but healed of the destructive memetic virus implanted in her youthful vulnerable spirit. Her message about the various forms of systemic and situational evil that are still among us in various masks is as vital today as it was in the try anything new era of the 70's. I especially valued her "song book" that guides us through each of her challenging chapters.

~Philip Zimbardo, Ph.D.
Professor Emeritus Stanford University
*The Lucifer Effect: Understanding
How Good People Turn Evil*

As a young girl, Diane Benscoter joins the cult of the Moonies and surrenders her life, will, birth family and vision of reality. There are adventures, chases, lies, arrests, and imprisonment. After a period of questioning and deep pain, the author emerges at the other side of her experience. Honest and courageous, *Shoes of a Servant* is a thoughtful examination of the forcible submission of an individual to the strictures of a religious cult. Thank you, Diane, for allowing us to understand and accompany you on this unusual and dangerous journey, and for writing this book.

~Kathleen Spivack- Writer, teacher.
With Robert Lowell and His Circle.

Shoes of a Servant is a captivating first-person account of a young woman's journey into the "Moonie" cult and her subsequent experience as a deprogrammer. This is an important book providing insight into the dangers of mind control. Her story is as relevant today as it was 30 years ago. I highly recommend it.

~Steven Alan Hassan M.Ed. LMHC, NCC
*Freedom of Mind: Helping Loved Ones Leave
Controlling People, Cults and Beliefs*

Shoes of a Servant is a great read. You won't be able to put it down. More importantly; as you read Diane's story of dedicating herself wholeheartedly to what she painfully learned was a manipulative lie, you will understand how imperative it is to teach the lessons within this book to young and vulnerable people. Read this book and share it with everyone - because everyone is vulnerable. I know this first hand since I worked with the police in the Matamoros Narco-Satanic case.

~Dr. Joachim De Posada
Don't Eat the Marshmallow...yet

Born in Nebraska, the author tells the gripping story of joining the world-wide Unification Church at the impressionble age of seventeen; then, for the next seven years, travelling with fellow "Moonies," to small towns and cities across the United States in order to help the Church and its Father/ Founder, the millionaire, Rev. Moon. A well told and true memoir.

~Hannelore Hahn
Founder of The International
Women's Writing Guild, 1976-2011.
On the Way to Feed the Swans

Shoes of a Servant
My Unconditional Devotion to a Lie

Diane Benscoter

A Lucky Bat Book

Shoes of a Servant
Copyright © 2013 Diane Benscoter
Cover Design Copyright © 2013 Nuno Moreira

ISBN 978-1-939051-37-0

Published by
Lucky Bat Books
LuckyBatBooks.com
10 9 8 7 6 5 4 3 2 1

I began this project as a letter, written to my mother, to thank her for loving me through the pain my journey caused her, and for persisting until I was free from "the lie." Although she passed away before this book was completed, I am comforted in knowing she read the original letter and was always able to read, across miles and time, the contents of my heart. I dedicate this book to her.

CONTENTS

PREFACE

IF YOU SEE YOURSELF, or someone you know between these pages, don't be surprised. This book tells a story that took place during a time of social change. Cults like the one I was in were fairly common in America during the '70s. I decided to tell my story not to address the issue of cults, as much as to expose a human condition and to shed light on extremism.

The human mind is susceptible to exploitation. Under certain conditions, the pathways leading to the part of the brain where rational thought takes place can be detoured to an area where nearly inescapable circular logic controls cognitive processes.

The words "never again" have come from many of our lips. History is filled with examples of atrocities carried out by groups of people swept up by extremist ideas. Extremism today takes the form of suicide bombers as well as various acts of violence born from hateful messages of "us versus them," propagated by opportunists seeking power or money.

Tens of thousands of troops cannot stop extremism. It is time we stopped looking for some vague enemy called "evil"—which we will never find—and start looking at the real cause of extremism: human vulnerability.

Memetics is an increasingly popular theory that addresses how ideas are spread from mind to mind. It has helped me create a framework for my experience. As you read my story, you will see how my cognitive processes were infected with a memetic virus created by someone claiming to be God. It is necessary to expose those who spread messages that further their quests for power and/or money at the expense of others.

These opportunists build viral memes in the name of their cause and seek out those most susceptible. For these memes or memeplexes to "go viral," certain cultural conditions must exist as well as a level of individual vulnerability in those it affects. The power of these kinds of memes are decreased by shedding light on how the brain can be tricked into cognitive detours leading away from rational thought.

Research must be done to identify the characteristics that contribute to the kind of vulnerability and loss of rational thought you will see in me as you read this book.

I didn't end up drinking poison in Guyana or strapping a bomb to my body. However, the memeplex controlling my cognition was equally as powerful as the ones that influenced others who have done such things. The youthful vulnerability that made me susceptible is chillingly common.

ACKNOWLEDGMENTS

OVER A DECADE HAS PASSED since I began writing this book. As I think back on those years, my strongest emotion is gratitude.

I am grateful that my daughter, Camille, is free from the kind of manipulation I experienced. Watching her finish high school and go on to college, seeing her develop as an individual and become a beautiful, strong young woman was something my mother didn't get to experience with me. My concern for my daughter and my empathy toward what my mother went through inspired me to tell this story.

I thank Hannelore Hahn, who founded the International Women's Writing Guild. She and her daughter, Elizabeth Julia Stouman, worked tirelessly to support women writers, regardless of their level of experience or portfolio. Had I not discovered the Guild during the time they were at the helm, this book would not exist.

Many wonderful teachers and friends from the Guild have provided immeasurable support and guidance.

Kathleen Spivack has been my mentor, teacher and friend throughout the writing of this memoir. It was at her insistence that I took on the project. She was emphatic that it was an important story to tell after our first conversation. She pushed me just beyond my comfort zone, and at the same time, always had my back. I am forever grateful to her.

Rachel de Baere has been my primary editor. Thank goodness! Her love of the craft of writing is contagious and I grew as a writer because of her. She edits with attention to detail, but never without kindness. While it's hard to see a manuscript marked up with corrections, there were always those places along the side that said things like "This is beautiful, sweetheart" that kept me going.

Dionne Fox offered encouragement and friendship from the book's inception and also helped with editing early drafts. Yael Flusberg has played the role of editor, life coach, and above all, dear friend. Mead Hunter also provided excellent editing.

The publishing industry has changed dramatically in recent years and I was fortunate to find Lucky Bat Books to help me through the changing landscape. I want to specifically thank Judith Harlan and Louisa Swann who have been my guides and partners through the publishing process.

My family has been waiting patiently for this book since before I began writing it. They have always believed in it, even when I was discouraged.

And finally I am grateful to Kim, who has listened patiently and offered suggestions that have always been insightful. She has loved me through difficult times and held me as my heart broke from the loss of my mother. Hers is the hand I will hold as I release this memoir.

Introduction

PREPARING TO TELL THIS STORY is like being in labor with my contractions growing more frequent as I struggle to begin. I close my eyes and press my fingers into my forehead, trying to push out the memories. *What were the words to those songs we sang,* I ask myself? They don't come. *If only I could get my hands on a songbook,* I think. I stare at the screen of my computer, which taunts me to write the first words. I can picture the blue book that was divided into two sections, "Inspirational Songs" and "Holy Songs."

Somewhere, packed downstairs, are a couple of boxes of deprogramming material. There are quite a few "Moonie" books there. These were the publications I read over and over when I was a follower of the notorious Sun Myung Moon, founder of the Unification Church to which I belonged. Since that was my area of specialization as a deprogrammer, I had saved them to use during deprogrammings, but I know there isn't a songbook among them. A friend with whom I used to work on Moonie rescues had one he would bring with him, but it's been over 20 years since we have spoken. And it's not as if I could order one from Amazon. Only members of the group have those books.

I decide to try searching the Internet. After several strings of search terms, I find myself on the official website of the Unification Church. I dig around and find a section containing words to "Holy Songs" and among them is the song I'm looking for: "Song of the Heavenly Soldiers." It's one of the songs we referred to as "fight songs." We sang them before heading out to do our work

—which was typically either selling candy or flowers, or trying to recruit new members.

As I read the words to the chorus, I softly sing the familiar tune and memories begin to emerge. With a clenched right fist, swinging our right arms, elbows bent, fervently stopping in front of our chest with each beat, we would sing those words at the top of our lungs. We were God's heavenly soldiers; the destiny of humanity was in our hands.

Besides the songbook, the website contains speeches by Moon, a bookstore, photos and various writings by members. There is so much to take in, all of which helps open passages to my memories, passages blocked by more than two decades of avoidance. At midnight the clock chimes and I take a deep breath. I know that I won't be getting much sleep. It feels like I have fallen into quicksand as I navigate the website.

I eventually discover a page within the site with contact information of current members; some of the members have links to their personal websites. The palms of my hands begin to sweat. Is it possible Crystal's name could be there, after all these years? The cursor hangs over "J" for a few seconds; finally I click on it. There it is, Ben and Crystal Johnson. I had heard they had gone back. A link is available next to their name. Again I click.

I am looking at the face of my dear friend. Or at least she used to be. The screen displays pictures of a family photo album. I stare at Crystal's face in the top picture. Seated next to Ben, their family surrounds them. The aging in their faces, especially Crystal's, is hard to accept. She had such a baby face when I saw her last. Now she looks like a grandma, which apparently she is.

Crystal was my spiritual parent—a title given to her for introducing me to the teachings of Sun Myung Moon—but I thought of her as a best friend or sister. We referred to everyone in the organization as our "brothers and sisters;" we were part of the "True Family" and Moon and his wife were the "True Parents." But Crystal felt more like a real sister to me than anyone else in the organization, even though we were assigned to missions that separated us during most of my time as a member.

My early bond with her, during my first few months after joining, had meant so much to me. Crystal stayed close during that time, teaching me as much as she could about my new life. Her devotion to the True Parents and her excitement about having found the Family was infectious. I remember her as childlike, maybe because she was still a child. We were among the youngest members then, both 17, another reason I felt so close to her.

To someone who hasn't been inside a cult, Crystal's picture on the website looks like any family photo. A Christmas tree stands in the background. The oldest sons, little boys when I last saw them, are obviously married now. They stand behind the couch, each with an arm around his wife. Three boys sit on the ground and there are two girls, one on either side of Crystal and Ben, sitting on the couch with them. I think maybe the girls are grandchildren, but they seem a little too old. Exploring the website further, I come to realize the girls are their youngest children, for a total of eight.

The Johnson family lives in a world that would be difficult for most people to understand. It's one in which everything is viewed through the filter of Moon's teachings. Since he is the Messiah, to question or contradict anything Moon says can only be interpreted as evil, wrong, or satanic.

To them, I betrayed God. I am on the side of Satan.

The visceral effect of seeing Crystal again surprises me; I'm twitching with adrenaline. The quicksand that has mired me since finding the lyrics to the fight song pulls me now with even greater force. I am sucked into the website, deeper into forgotten memories.

There is a photo album for each child. I want to look at them all, but my eyes stop on a picture of Crystal at the bottom of the page. She sits in front of the big brick house in Omaha where I first lived when I joined the group. She must have been about 16 at the time. I click on that picture. There are subheadings with groups of photos attached to each. One is titled "1974—50 mile walk." It's the "Walk for World Peace," which was my introduction to the group. A keystroke later, photos of the walk with me in them appear. I want to scream at the young me in the image, *run, and go home!*

One picture is of a group of us standing in front of the house holding handmade signs. Suddenly the memory of that day is so vivid I can almost feel the chill in the air.

My sign has the words "One World Crusade" handwritten on it. I have long wavy strawberry blonde hair and am wearing a stocking hat and gloves. I try to remember the name of the girl holding the sign with the words "World Peace..." Cathy, that's it, and her brother, Kyle, is holding a sign that says "Omaha to Des Moines." A poster with Sun Myung Moon's picture on it, announcing his speaking tour, is the biggest placard of all.

The clock chimes 1:00 a.m., and I begin to feel my sleepiness. I have looked at every picture on the Johnson family site, putting the pieces of their lives together as best I can. I am now acutely aware of how my life would have been so very different—had I not been deprogrammed.

I spend many hours in the following days, reading through pages of doctrine-filled documents and looking at photos on the website. Emotions and thoughts flow through me in layers. The surface layer finds much of what I read laughably ridiculous.

At the same moment though, another layer exists. As an ex-member, my past familiarity with the movement evokes vivid memories. I understand how intelligent people get to the place where they can believe irrational things—such as Moon being the Messiah—and how easy it can be to live a life built on and fed by lies and deceit. I find myself empathizing with the members still inside the Unification Church; even now I relate to the words that are part of their insiders' language. I can smell the sweet dirt-like aroma of treasured ginseng tea packets from Korea, which we only got to drink on special occasions. And I distinctly remember looking at a picture of Reverend Moon, the True Father, and his wife, the True Mother, every night before going to sleep. The photograph became tattered over the years, but I continued to stare at it daily, anticipating the day when the world would realize that the savior was on earth.

On yet another level, as I read and look at pictures, I experience a broader world perspective. I can understand why parents knowingly gave poison to their children in Jonestown, how jihad can be used to justify strapping a bomb onto your body and detonating it, how genocide can happen.

I ACCEPTED THE IDEA that Sun Myung Moon was the Son of God. He was one with the creator of all things, and I couldn't possibly understand God's plan without him. At that point, logic no longer functioned in a rational way. We were outside the laws of the country, because they were laws of man, not God. Anything could be rationalized: hurting the ones we loved, lying about the purpose of our fundraising, and tax evasion were just necessary evils supporting a higher good. Everyone would understand one day why Sun Myung Moon should choose everyone's mate, why women should never be leaders and why Moon lived lavishly while members like me sacrificed everything. God had a plan. There was a chilling relief in giving up my autonomy to someone I believed was God. To simply walk, as I pledged over and over, in the shoes of a servant, freed me of life's complexity.

With God leading the way, a vision of utopia becomes possible. What I didn't realize was that the vision requires blinders and with it the possibility of atrocities likes Jonestown.

FOR THE NEXT COUPLE WEEKS at my computer, I came back to those Web pages. Day after day, I befriended the young me and encouraged her to tell her story. More than twenty years have passed as I have grappled with trying to more clearly understand how I so willingly became a slave in the Moon organization.

As I look at the information about what's currently going on in the group, it's easy to see what has changed and what has not. There has been a definite shift in priorities from the time I joined. Now, with second and third generation Moonies, there seems to be a big focus on controlling those generations and exerting the teachings within the family unit, utilizing home schooling. There appears to be less of a focus on growing the membership through outreach and witnessing. It is less like a movement, as it was when I was a member, and more like a private club.

After spending many days reading speeches and online books, I eventually feel I have seen the majority of what I can find on the Web. I am repeatedly drawn back to the pictures of 17-year-old me. I was so young and full of optimism and idealism, about to begin a much longer walk than I ever planned on taking.

I see that same innocence and vulnerability in my own teenage daughter's beautiful smile. I want her to experience life to its fullest, to understand how to avoid the manipulation and destructive tactics to which I fell prey. I hope that through the telling of my story, a greater understanding of such dangers will be revealed.

A NOTE ABOUT THE CHAPTER TITLES. Music in general, and specifically the lyrics to songs, became a lifeline for me during the years of my life in which this book takes place. If I could play the songs for you before each chapter I would. They are the soundtrack of the book. If you don't know the songs, I hope you will listen to them.

PART ONE

FIVE YEARS AS A DISCIPLE

CHAPTER 1

WHAT'S GOING ON

Marvin Gay

I DROPPED OUT OF HIGH SCHOOL in 1973 when I was 16 years old. I had skipped so much school that quitting was more of a formality and a relief than a major event. The classes didn't seem to have anything of value to offer me. My parents had tried everything they could think of to get me "back on track," but nothing seemed to work. As happens with many teenagers, I felt no one understood me.

A few years prior, I had loved riding my yellow 10-speed bike around my little town. I enjoyed going to school, then coming home and talking on the phone for hours with my friends, gossiping and laughing together. I thought my family was the best in the world. But with adolescence, I started to feel like I didn't fit in. I began to realize that I didn't want to be the girl my parents wanted me to be. I could not see myself marrying the boy down the street and raising a family in Nebraska.

I wanted to do something about Vietnam and couldn't see how anyone was just going on with his or her life when such a horrible thing was happening. After a few fruitless attempts at sharing my thoughts with friends, I gave up trying to find someone to talk with about the things on my mind, and instead got high and listened to music. Drugs numbed my panic about knowing I didn't fit into my world anymore. I needed to get out of York, Nebraska, but hadn't yet figured out how.

I found solace in lyrics to songs by Cat Stevens, Bob Dylan and other songwriters, who wrote with passion about issues like war. Whoever wrote those songs understood what was important. I desperately wanted to find the kind of people who cared about the things in the lyrics to the songs I clung to like a security blanket as I fell asleep at night, my eight-track by my side. They didn't seem to live in my little town. I decided my life goal was traveling to see all that the world had to offer. I had heard of communal living and liked the idea. Maybe I could find a commune to join for a while. I knew I wouldn't need an education for that.

The population of York was only about 8,000 and it was the county seat—big, compared to some of the neighboring towns. I would walk to the A&W or the Ace Drive-In to meet up with friends and see where the party was. If there wasn't a "kegger" somewhere, we would make our own party by piling in someone's car and driving around the country roads.

The roads all looked pretty much the same. You could point the car in any direction and in one mile there would be a stop sign and a road crossing. This created neat little squares that looked like a quilt, from a plane. It went on like that for miles and miles. Most of the ditches had Budweiser cans decorating them and many of the road signs had dents from BB guns. There were no rivers or streams or even rolling hills, just cornfields and soybean fields with sprinkler systems running through them as far as the eye could see, broken up by the occasional farmhouse. Most of the houses were white with a big barn nearby and a silo standing tall to store the harvest. A couple of pick-up trucks and some farm machinery would sit parked around the property. I knew for sure I would never live in one of those houses.

I decided to start my search for a new life by moving to Lincoln, the capitol of Nebraska and a college town. I had gone to a number of concerts there and it seemed to have a lot going on, at least compared to York. It was close enough that I could stay in touch with my friends, but it felt like a fresh start. I moved in with a couple of girls from York who had been in my older brother, Bryce's, class.

The agreement with my parents was that I had to look for a job or get back into school. If one of those things didn't happen, I would have to move back in with them. I wasn't going to let that happen. I was ready to leave York and not look back.

The first few weeks in Lincoln, I wandered around, exploring the city, lonely and anxious to find something to do with my life that felt right. Many hours and whatever money I had I spent at a record store/head shop near the campus. I flipped through hundreds of records, not wanting to miss out on anything that might be revealed in the lyrics inside those album covers.

The idea of either working for some company to do something that meant nothing to me, or going to school just to get a diploma, a piece of paper that didn't prove anything, felt like two different versions of death.

I read all of the notes stuck on bulletin boards and stopped to read every poster I came across, picked up free or alternative newspapers and sat on park benches or under trees reading them. I wanted to know about every upcoming event and looked for clues that might lead me to the kind of people who wrote those songs that meant so much to me.

There was one particular alternative newspaper that was especially interesting. While reading it one morning, an inspiration came to me: *Maybe I could become a writer for them.* This would be a way to make a difference in the world. I found the address of the office where the paper was printed and decided to go there that afternoon to talk with them. Relieved that I had a plan, I started singing one of my favorite songs to myself. "O-o-h Child."

I had promised my roommate Sharon that I would meet her downtown at lunchtime—she was trying to help me get a job at the department store where she worked—so I started heading that way. I would go to the newspaper office after that. As I was on my way to meet her, a white van pulled over near where I was walking and several people jumped out of the back. There were boxes of bananas in the back of the van. The bananas had flyers wrapped around them, held on with rubber bands. The people who jumped out of the van started handing

the bananas out on the street. I took one, even though I wasn't
hungry. The guy who handed it to me tried to get me to stop
and talk, but there was no time. Already late to meet Sharon,
I barely slowed down to accept his offering or to say thanks. I
smiled and kept singing to myself.

When I met up with Sharon, 15 minutes late, I gave her the banana and read the flyer. It read: "Walk for World Peace. Please join us
for a 3-day walk to hear Reverend Sun Myung Moon speak in Des
Moines, Iowa. Food and housing provided. Bring a change of clothes,
a sleeping bag, good shoes and good cheer." There was a phone number and address at the bottom. I stuck the paper in my pocket.

Sharon was upset when I told her I wanted to try to get a job
writing for a newspaper, instead of working at the department
store where she worked. "I already talked to my manager. He is
expecting to meet you tomorrow," she said in a disapproving tone.

As she looked at me, her eyes filled with judgment. The needle following the groove on the record playing in my head was
rudely ripped from the vinyl and "Ooh Ooh Child" stopped. Old
feelings of not fitting in made me want to run away. I glanced to
the side and saw our reflection in the window of the building. She
was wearing a skirt and blouse and had platform shoes on. Her
blouse was cobalt blue with a white collar and cuffs. Her skirt was
slightly above the knee and had a plaid pattern, blue and white,
perfectly matching her blouse. Her hair was held back with a clip
and every strand was in place. Her make-up looked like she had
taken application tips from a magazine: there were two shades of
blue eye shadow in subtle layers, and she wore light pink lipstick,
perfectly applied. Everything was in fashion.

I was wearing a peasant shirt made of cheesecloth under my
suede jacket and bell-bottom jeans, which had several patches
sewn on them. I had Frye boots on, which were my favorite. They
were light brown with a small heel and rounded toe. My strawberry blonde hair was long, almost to my waist, and parted in
the middle. It was thick and wavy and fell in my face a lot. I was
wearing hoop earrings and also had some blue eye shadow on, but
didn't wear a lot of make-up and never took much time applying

it. I had taken a puff of pot not long before, so my eyes were a bit bloodshot. I just couldn't imagine working inside that building trying to look anything like Sharon.

"If the paper doesn't work out I still want to work with you," I lied. "I just have to try this." After a strained silence, I added, "At least you got a free banana." She chuckled, and I felt relieved. Even though Sharon rarely bent any rules, I knew part of her liked me because she could live vicariously through me. I added a little bit of wild to her life. I also knew that she somehow felt responsible to "straighten me out."

She peeled the banana and started eating it. "I'm on a new diet. This can be my lunch," she said. We sat on a bench for a while, and then she had to go.

"I'll see you at home later," I said as she was leaving.

"Good luck with the newspaper," she said, walking away. I knew by the way her eyes darted around, not meeting mine, that she was just being polite.

As much as I hated the thought of working in a department store, I was almost out of money and knew there wasn't much time before my parents would run out of patience and force me to go back to school—or worse and unthinkable, make me move back to York. I headed for the newspaper office, determined to convince them to hire me.

The needle fell back into the groove of the vinyl. "Ooh Ooh Child" played again. Someday I would walk in the rays of a beautiful sun and the world would be brighter.

When I got there, everyone was rushing around and I had to wait around for the editor. When he finally arrived, he reluctantly agreed to talk to me. I went back to his office, which was small and messy. There were books and papers in piles on his desk and the floor, part of a sandwich that looked several days old, and a coffee cup that looked like it hadn't been washed—ever. There were rings around the inside of the cup like a slice out of a tree trunk, displaying its age.

"We don't hire our writers as employees," he explained when I told him why I was there. "We pay by the article." He was a tall, skinny guy with long brown hair and a beard. He must have sensed my desperation and seemed to want to give me a chance. "Do you have any ideas for a story?" he asked. Nervously I put my hand in the pocket of my jeans and felt the paper from the banana. An idea came to me, and I pretended I had been thinking about it for awhile. I noticed him looking at my breasts but ignored it.

"I was thinking of going on this Walk for World Peace. Maybe I could write about that."

"Let me see," he said. I handed him the paper. He rubbed his beard as he read it. "Bring me back a story and we'll see," he said, giving me a little pat on the back and a flirting smile. Someone came to the door and he excused himself as he left the room to go talk with her.

"I got the job!" I told Sharon when she got home from work. I was packing my things when she walked in my room, even though it was only Thursday and I wouldn't be leaving until Saturday.

"What? Where are you going?"

I told Sharon about the paper around the banana and how that was the way I "got the job." I had already called the phone number on the piece of paper. A girl named Crystal had answered the phone and was extremely friendly. She explained that the walk would start on Saturday from Omaha, but that a couple of vans would be going from Lincoln to Omaha the morning of the walk and that I could catch a ride. She gave me an address in Lincoln and said she would be there to meet me. She seemed really happy that I was coming.

Sharon gave me a ride to the house on Saturday morning. We had a hard time finding the address and I was worried about being late. It was a little white house on a hill in a low-income neighborhood.

"Are you sure about this?" Sharon asked before I got out of the car.

"I'm sure," I said. I felt like an undercover agent on my first mission. "Thanks for the ride. I'll see you when I get home."

CHAPTER 2

PEACE TRAIN
Cat Stevens

SOMEONE OPENED THE FRONT DOOR and waved at me as I was getting out of the car. There were people putting things in two vans parked in the driveway. Sharon drove off.

I carried my small suitcase and sleeping bag to the front door. It was a little chilly that morning, so I was wearing a suede fur-lined coat over a turtleneck sweater. I had packed a pair of corduroys and two more pairs of jeans, three or four shirts, underwear, a few toiletries and my notebook and pen for taking notes for the article. I had also packed a few joints.

Someone by the name of Dwight ran up and introduced himself. He was wearing a white shirt and a blue tie and his clothes didn't seem to fit him quite right. His hair was unfashionably short, above the ears. It matched his completely out of fashion clothes, but he was certainly friendly.

"Hi," he said, shaking my hand and smiling with an excitement that reminded me of Mickey Mouse greeting people at the entrance to Disneyland.

"Hi," I answered, taking my hand back. "I talked to Crystal on the phone."

"We're so happy you came. Crystal," he yelled. "Your guest is here."

Crystal came hurrying out of the house and invited me inside after giving me a similar enthusiastic greeting and handshake.

"I'll take that," Dwight said, reaching for my suitcase and sleeping bag. I gave him my things and he hurried off with them to the van.

Crystal had a scarf wrapped around her head, tied in the back, accentuating her round face and pudgy cheeks. She wore a white blouse with a bow that tied in the front and a wool skirt that came below her knees.

Inside the house, I was relieved to see some normal-looking people. A guy with shoulder-length hair stood next to a girl with long red hair. They looked like people I was used to hanging around with. Kyle and Cathy were brother and sister, and had just arrived a few minutes before me. I saw them looking at the door like they were considering leaving. Crystal introduced me to everyone, then Dwight came in and announced that everything was ready to go.

"Diane, you come with me, and Beth, why don't you come with me too," Crystal said. "Kyle and Cathy, you go with Jeff." A fairly heavy girl with short curly black hair, she sat on the couch fidgeting and biting her nails. She was obviously a guest too. We both went outside and climbed into a white van with Crystal. Dwight drove. A girl by the name of Maggie rode with us as well. She sat between Beth and me. Crystal sat in the front passenger seat.

The ride from Lincoln to Omaha was a little over an hour. Crystal led the conversation, which never subsided the entire trip. She wanted to know everything about Beth and me. Beth didn't have a lot to say, so Crystal concentrated on me. She seemed sincerely interested in my life and in my opinions. When I told her I wasn't in school and that I wanted to join a commune she exclaimed with delight, "That's great!" That meant a lot to me. There wasn't anyone I knew who thought it was all right that I wasn't in school.

"Oh, I think God has a plan for you," she said, like she knew something I didn't and could hardly keep herself from letting me in on the secret. Turned around in her seat the whole time we were driving she was completely engaged in the discussion.

Maggie would occasionally try to draw Beth more into the conversation. Beth would say a few things, and then Crystal would ask me another question. She asked me about God, but it wasn't like a Born Again Christian asking if I had accepted Jesus as my personal lord and savior. She wanted to know if I thought God had a plan to make the world better and if I thought God had a plan for my life. She seemed hopeful about changing the world, not saving my soul through accepting Jesus. She listened intently to every word I said, as if my opinion mattered. I opened up like an explosion, but by the time we got to Omaha I was feeling overexposed and hung over from adrenaline. Within an hour of meeting Crystal I had been more candid with her about my innermost thoughts than I remembered being with anyone ever before. I couldn't wait to get out of the van. I also really had to pee.

We pulled into an alley behind a house in Omaha just ahead of the other van. I quickly looked to make sure Kyle and Cathy were there. They made me feel safe, like I hadn't completely left behind everything I was familiar with. They were there.

I asked to use the restroom the minute we were out of the van. Crystal guided me in through a gate and down a short path to the back door of the house. We went through a kitchen and into a dining room. It smelled as if something was baking. She pointed down a hallway to a door.

When I came out she was waiting by the door. I thought she was waiting for the bathroom, but she was waiting for me. "I want you to meet someone," she said. I followed her back down the hallway past the dining room. A girl with short brown hair wearing a long blue skirt and a flowered shirt was setting a big plate of muffins and a bowl of fruit on the table in the dining room. Everyone from the two vans had gathered in the dining room and Dwight was offering food and tea or juice to everyone. I was starting to get hungry and those muffins smelled good, but I followed Crystal around the corner. There were some people sitting on the floor in the living room making posters and signs.

A dark-complected man wearing a suit and tie that actually fit him was coming down some stairs toward us. He greeted us with a smile. He was in his early thirties and handsome.

"Lokesh, I want you to meet Diane. Diane, this is Lokesh," she said, almost giddy with excitement.

Lokesh took my hand, and then wrapped his other hand around my hand as if I were his precious friend. "I'm so happy to meet you," he said, holding on to my hand a second or two longer than I expected. "Did you get some food?" He motioned to the dining room. He sat down and offered me a chair next to him. "Get some food, please, you must be hungry." I took a muffin and poured myself some juice.

Crystal brought a china cup of tea with milk in it to Lokesh. Everyone else was drinking out of Styrofoam. He took a sip. "Perfect. Thank you," he said to Crystal. She looked proud.

Crystal sat on his other side and proceeded to tell him all about me. He listened intently, asked me a few questions about where York was and how many people were in my family, and then politely excused himself after a short time. Soon Crystal excused herself as well. Walking toward Kyle and Cathy, Jeff intercepted me and talked with me until someone announced that we were about ready to go.

A flurry of action began. Dwight and Crystal handed out signs and took posters to the van and attached them to the sides. The walk was scheduled to take us five days. We needed to cover about 30 miles each day. We stood in front of the house for photos, holding our signs, and then headed out. It seemed like it took us hours just to get out of Omaha. It was cold out, but it helped to be walking at a fairly good pace.

Loudspeakers were attached the top of one of the vans, with posters taped to the sides announcing the "Walk for World Peace." Dwight was inside playing guitar and singing folk songs like "If I Had a Hammer" and "Blowing in the Wind" over the speaker system between announcements about the walk. He kept making the point that the Unification Church and the One World Crusade were sponsoring the walk. I didn't pay much attention to what he was saying though and wished he would talk less. What impressed me was how he could make his 12-string guitar sound.

The media came at one point. They took pictures and talked to Lokesh, who was leading the walk. The excitement the members expressed was contagious in spite of my uneasiness with how strange and out of sync with society they all seemed. The way they dressed was enough to characterize them as odd. I was glad it was cold because we were all wearing coats, making them look a little more normal—still not "cool," but it was less embarrassing to be seen with them. I continued to try to work my way closer to the other guests on the walk, feeling like they would be easier to talk to. However, members intervened by starting conversations with me and with the other guests, interfering with my efforts.

We walked bunched into one group through the city, about 15 of us, but began to spread out more once we were on the country roads and had put the signs in the van. We brought them out and carried them when we came to towns.

One of the members, Jake, walked with me that first day for what seemed like most of the day. I found him boring and irritating. He was a big guy, at least a foot taller than me. He had long legs and walked faster than I wanted to go. He talked the whole time. It wasn't that the things he was saying weren't interesting. He talked about how the world would be better if we were one big family, and about how meeting this group had changed his life. It was sort of like he was teaching a class instead of having a conversation. Plus he kept sniffing and rubbing snot on his sleeve. I kept thinking about the joints in my pocket.

Finally we stopped for lunch. We sat in the van together and ate sandwiches and bananas. Nowhere near a bathroom, I realized I needed one—as well as a break from these people. I quietly asked Cathy, one of the non-members, if she would walk with me into some nearby woods to find a place to go. We took off before anyone else could decide that they wanted to come along. Dwight yelled for us to hurry back as we walked off.

I immediately told Cathy that I had some joints and we took a few puffs. When we got back it was time to get going. Jake walked toward us. I saw Crystal and went over to ask her how far we still had to go that day, and to avoid more time with Jake. She walked with me for most of the rest of the day along with another group member, Jeff. The theme of the conversation was a continuation of the one with Jake—utopia.

As we walked, Crystal and Jeff started to seem less weird to me. They asked me lots of questions about my family and my life, but mostly about how I envisioned the ideal world. I wasn't used to walking that far and was tired, but as the miles passed I cared less about how tired I was and wanted to know more about the group they were part of—partly for the article I was planning to write and partly because I was interested in living in a commune and they seemed to live like a big family.

I liked Jeff. He was kind of a regular guy. He didn't try too hard to impress me, and even though he had short hair like all the guys in the group, his mannerisms made him easier to be around. He joked around about sore feet and talked about the scenery along the way, all with no apparent agenda. It seemed like the others never said anything that didn't somehow have to do with God or the work they were doing to change the world.

Crystal's foot started to bother her, so she rode in the van for a while and Dwight took her place walking with me. We talked about music. He knew a lot of the bands and songwriters I liked, and when I named specific songs like Led Zeppelin's "Stairway to Heaven" and "Nights in White Satin" by the Moody Blues, he promised to play them for me at some point.

Our route avoided the major freeways. Lokesh arranged ahead of time that we would sleep in little churches along the way. I listened closely as he talked to the ministers at a couple of the places we stayed, explaining to them some of the details about Reverend Moon's speaking tour. I wanted to use the information for the article I was going to write. He described Moon as a Christian evangelist who hadn't been in the U.S. for long. Lokesh described the Unification Church as a non-denominational Christian church founded in Korea. I wasn't sure how interesting of an article I would be able to write about them. I didn't see much of a story.

On the first day, when we finally arrived in Carson, Iowa, we had walked about 30 miles. The pastor of a small church welcomed us. The minister and his wife brought us soup and showed us where we could sleep. They were apologetic that all they had to offer was a place to sleep on the floor of the church basement.

Lokesh assured them we were very comfortable and thanked them again. He then announced that we would be hearing a lecture before bedding down. Dwight led us in some songs and played a couple of solo pieces that he had written for his 12-string guitar, which he played beautifully. Lokesh said a prayer and then began to lecture. He wrote on a blackboard while he talked. His demeanor was warm. Although he had grown up in India, his English was perfect and he spoke with confidence and charm.

The lecture opened with an introduction of the Divine Principle, the teaching of Sun Myung Moon. We were all so tired it was hard to sit and listen to a lecture. Lokesh made it clear that he was presenting a revelation Sun Myung Moon had received directly from God and that it explained the fundamental questions of life.

Everything he said made sense to me. "We all want to be happy; it is a universal fact," he explained, and then gave examples both of what the world should be like and how it fell short. He went on to define happiness as a union between body and mind, man and woman, God and man, and ultimately humankind and the universe. I looked around the room. The members were all paying close attention, laughing at his subtle jokes, shaking their heads yes or no based on what he said. The main point was that the struggles individuals have within themselves are similar to universal struggles. Something happened to cause a fundamental problem in the world and whatever that was cut us off from our true nature and from God. The good thing, Lokesh said, was that God had a plan to fix the problem and that plan was revealed to Reverend Moon.

The conversations of the day, all the discussions about utopia were now being presented from an academic and theological perspective, neither of which I had been exposed to before. Lokesh kept it short that night, and though the other guests were falling asleep, he had gotten my attention. I wanted there to be an answer that would explain everything and guide us toward world peace.

Though exhausted from walking all day, I fell asleep that night feeling excited. I thought about the article I was there to write and wondered if I should take a few minutes to jot down some of my thoughts about the day, but it seemed less important than rest. I decided to work on it when I woke up.

The next day, we took off early after eating muffins and fruit, brought from Omaha. There was no time to write. My legs were sore from the day before and it seemed like we would never arrive at the place we were scheduled to stay that night. The scenery didn't change much as we walked along the highway. There were occasional small groves of trees, but mostly flat farmland. We went through a couple of small towns and took out our signs as we walked through them. Ben walked with me most of that day. He was tall and lanky and reminded me of the Scarecrow from "The Wizard of Oz." We talked about the horrible state of the world and how wonderful it would be if we could learn to be one big family.

We walked 36 miles that day before arriving at the tiny town of Massena. I kept dozing off during the lecture that night. When it was time for sleep, I got my notebook out but fell asleep with it open to an empty page next to my pillow, pen in hand.

We started early again on the third day. There was plenty of time to talk about the previous night's lecture in great detail as we walked—a somewhat shorter distance, fortunately. Crystal walked with me for most of the day and Lokesh joined us for a while. Kyle walked with us in the afternoon, discussing biblical scriptures as they related to the lecture the night before. Kyle obviously cared deeply about the Bible and knew a great deal about it. He told Lokesh he was a Born Again Christian. I felt less like he was someone I could relate to than I did the first day, when I had hoping he was more of a hippie.

The second night's lecture was about the biblical story of the fall of man. During this lecture, Lokesh revealed the "true" meaning of the symbols and metaphors in the Bible as they pertained to the story of Adam and Eve. According to Reverend Moon's revelation, it was an act of sex that took place, not merely the eating of fruit. I didn't really care if it was fruit or sex. My family was Methodist. For me, church was more social than religious.

Whatever Lokesh claimed was true, I was sure, must be true. Even Kyle, who seemed skeptical at the beginning of the conversation, was getting excited about how much sense this new interpretation seemed to make.

I wanted to hear more about this group, to which they all belonged. Especially intriguing was the fact that they were international. Still wanting to travel to different parts of the world, I began to wonder if this could be a way for me to do that. I didn't tell them I was interested in getting involved if I could travel, but I was hoping to find out more about how that might work. I knew there was plenty of time, so I listened to the discussions while my mind wandered with the fantasy of seeing the world. When I got the chance, I snuck off and smoked a little more of my joint.

That third night the lecture moved on to the life of Jesus. There was also a history lecture that explained how God had been working throughout human history to restore his children to their original state, before the fall of man in the Garden of Eden. I later learned that the lectures we heard were abbreviated from the version that was usually presented, because we were all so tired by the time Lokesh spoke each night. Still, he seemed to be leading us through a lot of information about what the Bible really meant.

Kyle was starting to annoy me. He had changed, for me, from a long-haired hippie and potential buddy to get high with into a Jesus freak. He continued to ask questions, often disagreeing with what Lokesh said, especially about things related to the Bible. Lokesh seemed to anticipate and welcome his questions, and Kyle ultimately seemed satisfied with the responses. The longest discussion was about Jesus failing his mission. Lokesh reframed the concept over and over. It wasn't that Jesus himself was a failure; the mission he came here to complete was a failure, Lokesh explained. It happened because of circumstances, especially having to do with failings of his followers. Jesus's death on the cross should not have happened. Instead, he should have created the Kingdom of Heaven on earth. That, according to Reverend Moon's revelation from God, was Jesus's mission. This made sense to me. And if I could understand it, I wondered what was wrong with Kyle.

I could tell that Kyle was still skeptical, but everyone was tired and I was happy to end the discussion and go to bed that night. I decided it would be best to write the article when I got home.

Beth was having problems with the amount of walking we did every day and sometimes went to bed instead of listening to the lectures. Maggie seemed to be taking care of her. I heard them talking as we walked sometimes. Maggie would explain to Beth everything she had missed the night before. They rode in the van a good part of the distance.

The lecture series began to weave a tale that seemed to be completely backed up with biblical scriptures and historical events. It included timetables with specific dates that demonstrated God's exact process, leading us to the current day. It was becoming obvious that we were living in a time God had been working towards since Jesus's death.

We were getting closer to Des Moines, so I decided to start asking questions about how an interested person would go about joining the group. I didn't have a high school diploma and wondered what the requirements were to join. I had heard about the Peace Corps and wondered if this was something like that. Crystal told me to wait until I heard the final lecture tonight and then we could talk about it. I was beginning to see beyond the clothes and haircuts and to know these were good people who really cared about making a better world. I couldn't wait to meet members from other countries.

On the night before we were to arrive at our destination, Lokesh presented the "Conclusion" lecture. By then, I had come to think of Lokesh as the most intelligent person I had ever met. He seemed to know everything there was to know about the Bible and all of history.

Lokesh started by reminding us how we all agreed the world should be more like one big family. Now, at last, through the revelation that Sun Myung Moon received from God, we could finally understand what had happened to cause all of the problems we see in the world today. We could understand how God had been working through specific timelines and laws to bring us back to that ideal world we all want. We also understood that the foundation had been set for the Messiah to finally return and that soon the Kingdom of Heaven on Earth would be possible.

He started writing on the blackboard. How would the Messiah arrive? Where would he arrive? Exactly when would he arrive? How would we know him? These were the questions in front of us that night. One by one, logical answers to the questions became apparent. Like solving a puzzle, the answers were teased out of us, but not completely.

The answer to the first question came from Lokesh pulling from scripture and showing us how God's laws, which we could now clearly understand from Moon's revelations, supported the scriptures. There was no question. The Messiah would come as a man, just like Jesus came as a man.

A key theme throughout the lectures we had been hearing had to do with what was referred to as the laws of indemnity. Those laws prescribed certain conditions that had to be met before God could take the next step toward us. Indemnity had to be paid when man sinned. Then, and only then, could the damage of sin be reversed. This law was demonstrated over and over throughout the lectures as the story of human history was told.

The idea of God working through numerology was another recurring theme. "God is an orderly God," Lokesh had pointed out. Each major point of God's dispensation had happened in exact time periods. Lokesh strongly emphasized the number of years between major events throughout the presentations. Using this logic, we could know when the Messiah would arrive. As the lectures brought us closer to current time, the answer became glaringly clear. The Messiah should have been born shortly after the First World War.

At this point, we all started looking at each other for reality checks. This meant he was on the earth now. I started to feel like I was on some sort of drug. There was so much adrenaline pumping through my blood. Christ was here! War would end! The world would be saved once and for all!

/here will he be born? Again scriptures were quoted. Lokesh ᴅ‿ ιn to write on the chalkboard and spoke with authority and conviction. He made a case that Christ could only be born in the East, in a Christian nation. He wrote Japan, China and Korea on the board, and then one by one gave reasons why Japan and China could not be the correct place for the birth of the second coming of Christ. He crossed out Japan and China. He would be born in Korea. He circled the word.

"How will we recognize him?" Lokesh asked. The silence was a little longer than was comfortable. "He will bring a revelation that will be the key to building the Kingdom of Heaven on earth." Kyle started to cry. Lokesh suggested that if we pray sincerely and ask God to help us understand, we would know where to look for the Messiah.

I didn't have to pray. I knew that I was on my way to meet Christ himself, the embodiment of God. I spent hours that night talking with Crystal. I wanted to know everything. And she wanted to tell me everything. She showed me pictures of Moon and his wife and explained that they were the True Parents. It was as if she was in love, as if they all were exploding with love for their Messiah. Even Lokesh seemed to change once we all knew the truth about whom we were on our way to see. He revealed a playful smile I hadn't seen before. I wanted to call home and tell my family, all my friends, everyone. Christ was here! I didn't have to wonder what to do with my life any longer or think about anything but following where the Messiah led me.

I was awake most of the night thinking of what it meant to be on the way to meet the savior of the world. I thought of the story of the three kings on their way to see baby Jesus. I decided that I wanted to bring a gift. When I told Lokesh, he suggested I give up something that I love, to show God my seriousness. I decided I should cut my hair.

I loved my hair. I thought of the woman who stopped me as I was walking, just a few days before coming on the walk. She complimented on how beautiful it was. Thick and wavy, it was also a symbol of being part of the counterculture. I loved long hair on guys and they seemed to love it on me. So now I would offer my most prized attribute to God.

Maggie cut my hair for me—at least a foot of it. I also decided to start a three-day fast. Crystal mentioned it to me as a possibility before I decided on the hair, so I thought it would be good to do both.

That day, I told Crystal about the article I had come on the walk to write. I thought that the article could be a way I could help get the word out about who Sun Myung Moon was. She warned me to take it slow and to keep in mind that God had a plan for me that I couldn't fully understand at that point. She suggested that maybe God had used that to get me to come on the walk, but that now everything was different.

That made sense to me. Everything did feel different. I was no longer a rebellious teenager from York, Nebraska, who might have to go to work in a department store. I was a disciple of the Second Coming of Christ.

The plan was to walk all the way to the house where Reverend Moon was staying during his time in Des Moines. His public speech was the same night we were due to arrive. As we came into the city of Des Moines, we pulled out the signs. It had started to snow and the wind was blowing. We had to cut holes in the signs so that we could hold them up against the wind. A van from a local TV station pulled up next to us as we were walking and asked to talk with us about our walk. Lokesh talked with them, which was great for publicity, but we were all worried about the time. We wanted to hurry and get to the house before Moon left to give his speech.

Everyone was brimming with excitement when we knew we were in the neighborhood where Moon was staying, especially Crystal, who was like a child about to meet Santa Claus. As we finally approached the house, we could see people standing outside waving to us. Among them was Sun Myung Moon, the man I would refer to as "Father" for the next five years.

He stood with a small group of other people in his immediate circle, including two of his children. They began to clap for us as we got closer. Crystal and Maggie started to run. They fell to the ground at Moon's feet in a full bow, heads to the ground. He touched their heads and invited us all into the house.

We entered a typical suburban home and sat on the floor in front of "Father and Mother," who were sitting in chairs. There was an interpreter there, a Korean woman, and various other people who came in and out of the room. A woman came around handing out cups of warm milk. I turned it down. Lokesh explained to the woman serving the milk, who had raised her eyebrows at my refusal, that I had just joined the day before and was fasting. He went on to explain to everyone in the room, all of whose attention had turned to him, that five people had joined during the walk. Father and Mother both seemed very happy about that. Their son, Hyo Jin, who was 11 at the time, sang for us. Dwight played the guitar for them and a couple other members sang to them. Through the interpreter, Moon talked about how he used to have to walk long distances in the snow.

We didn't stay long. Father needed to get ready for his public speech that evening. We rode in the van when we left the house, and on top of all the other emotions I was feeling, I was glad to be done with the walk. My feet were blistered and sore.

There wasn't much time to get ready to go to the speech. We drove to the Iowa "center" to change into nicer clothes. The center was a small house with a finished basement. We put our things downstairs and quickly changed into the best clothes we had. I hadn't brought anything very nice, but put on a sweater and some corduroy pants.

The turnout for the speech was smaller than I had expected. I somehow thought there would be droves of people. Everything was so huge in my mind. It was only a couple hundred people, at the most, barely filling up a small venue. I hadn't eaten all day and was weak from fatigue. I knew I was part of something that was more important than anything I had ever known, but I just wanted to sleep. We stayed that night and for the next two days with the Iowa "family."

All the members were busy taking care of the logistics involved with Moon's visit, but still someone was always close by, talking to me about the history of the church or the speaking tour or how great it was to be part of God's work. I stayed at the center the third day of my fast and rested. Everyone else was out selling flowers to raise money for the center. We could have come along and it sounded kind of fun, but I was really run down.

When the time came that I had completed a full three days of fasting, there was no one around except Cathy, one of the other new members who had asked if she could stay behind as well. She had caught a cold and needed to rest. I had a few dollars and went to the corner store and bought a candy bar and soda. Having never fasted before, I didn't know that was a bad way to break a fast. When the members arrived back at the center, I was in a lot of pain.

Crystal made me some rice and told me to eat a little bit at a time. I could tell she felt bad for not being there when it was time for me to break the fast. I felt very well cared for.

By the time we were in the van heading back to Nebraska, Crystal and I had talked about going to get my things and moving me into the house in Omaha. She had spoken with Lokesh and they decided it would be better for me to live at the Omaha center at first instead of at the center in Lincoln. I trusted their opinion about what was best for me. Omaha was an hour drive east of Lincoln and a much bigger city. I would be two hours from York—and a world away from my old life.

Lokesh sat down next to me in the dining room when we arrived back in Omaha and explained how special it was for me to have met the True Parents on the day I joined. The way he talked scared me a little. His tone was so serious, and I suddenly felt indebted to him for the experience. As time went by I realized what a badge of honor it all was. Throughout my years in the group, I almost always had the best "how did you join" story. Many members I met, even after many years inside the group, had never been anywhere near the True Parents or their children.

CHAPTER 3

HIGHER GROUND
Stevie Wonder

THERE WAS SPECIFIC TERMINOLOGY members used among themselves, and it didn't take me long to start to pick up on the language of the group. I was now part of "the family" and had "True Parents." Crystal was my spiritual mother because she had been my first contact with the group. All the women were sisters and the men were brothers. I was part of the Nebraska family, of which Lokesh was the head. Satan was the enemy and we were God's heavenly soldiers building the Kingdom of Heaven on earth. We had to leave everything behind us in order to fulfill God's will. Indemnity was needed to pay for past sins. I knew I had a lot to pay, and that as disciples, we were in the position to pay indemnity for the sins of our ancestors all the way back to Adam and Eve.

I was ready to get started. Now that the Messiah was on the earth, I didn't see any reason why we couldn't make the entire world see the light in a matter of a few years. Clearly, the Kingdom of Heaven was at hand.

One of the things I was excited about was that we were also going to restore the "spirit world," which is where everyone who had ever lived on the earth but then passed away was now living. Spirit world also included angels, who are not human. Satan was an angel, the Archangel Lucifer. Angels influenced our lives on a continuous basis, and could be good or bad, depending on whether they were working for God or Satan. It was our job to restore the spirit world in the same way as the world of the living. They would all eventually be part of the new Kingdom of Heaven. I couldn't wait until Janis Joplin, Jimi Hendrix and Jim Croce were part of the family. I was really looking forward to meeting them.

I called my roommates and my Mom the day after I got back to Omaha. My Mom sounded worried when I told her I had decided I was moving to Omaha with the group with whom I had gone on the Walk for World Peace.

"Honey, who are these people?" Mom asked. "Why would you move in with them? You just met them."

"You can come to a lecture, and then you'll understand." I said this three times during the conversation, with a smile in my voice, hardly able to contain my excitement, knowing she would soon understand that the Messiah was on the earth.

When I called Sharon and told her the news she was angry. This meant they had to find another roommate. I had been talking to Crystal and Lokesh about getting my things. I didn't have that much, but we decided to go to the apartment to get what I had that week.

Several members of my new family came along—Ben, Dwight and Maggie—to make sure things went all right. Sharon was in the apartment when we got there. She didn't bother with hello.

"What did you do to your hair?" She stared at my hair as if cutting it were a tragedy.

"I cut it." I couldn't go into why right then. I tried to talk to her about coming to a Divine Principle lecture, but she was in no mood to accept the invitation. She was fixated on my hair.

APRIL, MY OTHER ROOMMATE, came home while I was gathering my things. She was in a hurry to go somewhere and had only stopped in to change her clothes. She seemed really worried about me and surprisingly rude to Ben, Dwight and Maggie. April was usually a very sweet, polite person. She had won a statewide teen beauty contest when she was in high school and always carried herself with poise. She seemed like a big sister to me in that moment, even though I had never thought of her like that before. It made me feel good; even though she was being rude to the people I knew I needed to stay aligned with. She clearly didn't like the fact that I was moving out and didn't think the people I was moving in with had good intentions.

At one point, she asked me a question about where I was moving to in Omaha and Ben started to answer for me. "I wasn't asking you," she snapped at him.

I didn't know the address but I told her I would really like it if she would come to a lecture and dinner at my new home. Like Sharon, she wasn't interested at all.

During the ride back to Nebraska after the walk, I had made a list of everyone I was sure would immediately join the family. Sharon and April were both on the list. I couldn't believe that neither was willing to come to a lecture. I assumed that as soon as I told the key people in my life that I had discovered something great, they would immediately drop everything and come to see what it was. Then, I thought, they would join, like I had, the minute they heard the conclusion lecture.

As I was taking the last load of my things to the van, Sharon asked me if my Mom knew what I was doing.

"Don't worry, I called her," I said with obvious frustration. I gathered the last of my things. "You can have my records," I told her. The look on her face was of total disbelief. She knew how much my music meant to me. Now she looked more worried than angry. "You will understand soon," I told her as we were leaving.

I threw all of my poetry and journals in the trash along with most of my clothes and jewelry, which included a ring my grandma had given me made from my silver baby spoon. I was overcoming Satan. He wanted me to stay connected to things that would keep me from my mission. When I threw out my poetry and the ring it was like burning a bridge between my new life and the old me.

I had a long talk with Dwight about music before we went to get my things. I liked Dwight from the first time I heard him play the guitar and had talked with him a lot about music. He understood how important music was in my life, but he also knew that Satan was working to distort the truth and that music was a key vehicle for influencing young people away from God. In the new world, there would be great music. I knew it wouldn't be long before all my favorite musicians would understand the truth and join our family. Those records I had collected were filled with Satan's influence. The theme of sex and drugs that was woven through the songs was clearly Satan's efforts to promote his evil ways. They had to be left behind.

DURING THOSE FIRST FEW MONTHS living with the Nebraska family, I learned much more about Satan. He was a daily topic. The Divine Principle story of how Satan came to exist was much like a children's story. It told of how the archangel Lucifer had illicit sex with Eve. Eve then tempted and seduced Adam, and thus started the lineage of evil. Since everyone descends from Adam and Eve we have all inherited the original sin, according to the Divine Principle. The only way to fix it was to begin a new lineage of people. The Messiah's job was to begin that new lineage. I realized this was a different version of the Bible than I had been taught and that theologians disagreed with this interpretation, but academic comparisons of traditional interpretations of the story of Adam and Eve to the Divine Principle story didn't interest me much. This had to be the real version, because the Messiah was the voice of God. Why worry about some ancient translation of a book when we can simply ask God's true and living son?

The evidence of evil in the world was pointed out constantly. This answered so many questions that had plagued me, such as how there could be war. Now I knew it was all Satan's work. That was why I couldn't stay in school. I was being prepared by God to fight Satan. Before leaving York I had lain awake and cried in bed when I heard anti-war songs like Graham Nash's "Chicago/ We can change the World" or "One Tin Soldier," from the movie Billy Jack.

Now I had one word to explain how a tragedy like Vietnam could occur: Satan. I also knew there would be an end to Satan's evil work, since the Messiah was here. It didn't seem very complicated. All of the complications of the world fell into place in a comfortably simple closed loop in my mind. If it was bad, it was Satan; if it was good, it was God. Moon was the embodiment of God; if I did what he said, Satan would be defeated. That was all I really needed to know. Anything more complicated, I was sure had an explanation within the Divine Principle, which was always there to support that simple loop back to Moon having the final word. Our inherent sin made it such that we often got confused. Satan was part of our DNA and worked hard to confuse Moon's disciples. Fortunately, Moon didn't have that confusion to deal with, being without sin. It was all so simple and beautiful: Just follow the True Parents.

Continuously warned about Satan working through the people I loved, I began to understand better why it was so difficult for my biological family to accept God's truth. I was specifically chosen and prepared by God to receive the Divine Principle, but that didn't mean my family and friends were. It would take time. Satan's powers were strong and his main focus, since the advent of the Messiah, was to stop Moon's disciples from helping him succeed in his mission. After all, this was the same Satan that caused Judas to betray Jesus.

Even though I knew it would take longer than I had originally thought, I still wanted to do everything I could to persuade my friends and family to join. I imagined being close to my family again. I hadn't felt connected to them since I was in grade school. I remembered the feeling, though, and wanted it again—but this time, with everything I understood about the True Family at the center of our connection.

I felt at home in the Omaha center. The house was a square brick structure. It had three stories and a basement. The sisters' room was on the third floor. The stairwell leading up to that part of the house was steep and narrow. It felt like a secret area of the house; only sisters went up there. We slept on the floor in sleeping bags on top of thin foam mats. There was a closet full of blouses and skirts. Crystal gave me permission to borrow anything in there that fit until we could get me some suitable clothes. We were never to wear seductive clothes and took our cues from what the Korean and Japanese sisters wore. Our skirts were to be at least to the middle of the knee and our shirts had to be loose fitting and never show any cleavage.

When I moved in, five of us shared the room. Crystal went back and forth between the Lincoln Center and the Omaha Center. She and Dwight were in charge in Lincoln, but it was used more for a base to work from while they were in Lincoln than a full-scale center, like the Omaha Center was.

The brothers' room was on the second floor and had a similar set-up. There were six brothers sleeping in that room. Lokesh had a room of his own on that floor. Another smaller room toward the back of the house, also on that floor, was the prayer room. It was completely empty, except for a coffee table against the wall with a framed picture of the True Parents, standing together, with their heads bowed in prayer.

Rituals and prayer meetings took place in that room. On Sunday mornings at 5:00 a.m., on the first day of the month, and on Holy Days, we would gather in the prayer room for Pledge Service. It was a tradition that took place throughout the world, no matter what the circumstance; every member was expected to attend. We would bow to the picture three times, full bows, all the way on our knees with our foreheads touching the ground. Then we would recite "My Pledge" in unison. Whoever was leading the service, usually Lokesh, handed out small pieces of paper with these words on them.

MY PLEDGE

1. As the center of the cosmos, I will fulfill our Father's Will (purpose of creation), and the responsibility given me (for self-perfection). I will become a dutiful son (or daughter) and a child of goodness to attend our Father forever in the ideal world of creation (by) returning joy and glory to Him. This I pledge.

2. I will take upon myself completely the Will of God to give me the whole creation as my inheritance. He has given me His Word, His personality, and His heart, and is reviving me who had died, making me one with

Him and His true child. To do this, our Father has persevered for 6,000 years the sacrificial way of the cross. This I pledge.

3. As a true son (or daughter), I will follow our Father's pattern and charge bravely forward into the enemy camp, until I have judged them completely with the weapons with which He has been defeating the enemy Satan for me throughout the course of history by sowing sweat for earth, tears for man, and blood for heaven, as a servant but with a father's heart, in order to restore His children and the universe, lost to Satan. This I pledge.

4. The individual, family, society, nation, world, and cosmos who are willing to attend our Father, the source of peace, happiness, freedom, and all ideals, will fulfill the ideal world of one heart in one body by restoring their original nature. To do this, I will become a true son (or daughter), returning joy and satisfaction to our Father, and as our Father's representative, I will transfer to the creation peace, happiness, freedom and all ideals in the world of the heart. This I pledge.

5. I am proud of the one Sovereignty, proud of the one people, proud of the one land, proud of the one language and culture centered upon God, proud of becoming the child of the One True Parent, proud of the family who is to inherit one tradition, proud of being a laborer who is working to establish the one world of the heart.

I will fight with my life. I will be responsible for accomplishing my duty and mission. This I pledge and swear. This I pledge and swear. This I pledge and swear.

After the pledge, Lokesh would read an excerpt of a speech Father had given, which he had chosen ahead of time, and then we would have unison prayer followed by silent prayer. Unison prayer was a time when everyone would pray his or her own personal prayer, out loud, at the same time. It would become louder and more fervent by the minute, as each person competed to impress God (or the other people in the room) with their sincerity and commitment. For the silent prayer we got down on our knees again, often for a numerically important number of minutes, like 12 or 21. During the silent prayer there was often snoring in the room.

We ended with a "Holy Song." A pile of Holy Song books sat in a small pile in the room.

Sometimes, when we would sing certain songs, I cried. I knew other family members all over the world were singing the same words and that it wouldn't be long until everyone on earth knew that the Messiah was in our presence. I knew during those tearful moments that I would never leave the true family or betray the Messiah. I would spend my life working for father, in the shoes of a servant.

The master bedroom was also on that floor. The True Parents had stayed there once during a speaking tour, which had taken place about a year before I joined. The room had been completely remodeled and had all new furniture. This was done to accommodate them for the few nights they stayed. There was a private bath connected to the room. The bathroom had a second door, which opened to another smaller room with a single bed in it. Lokesh slept there. The furniture there was notably humbler.

The area where the True Parents had stayed had not been used since their stay. It was a shrine.

We had a small area in the sisters' bedroom where we kept our few personal items. I had a couple of photos of the True Parents that Crystal had given to me as gifts. Crystal kept her things in a small chest, and one day she showed me everything in it. There were photos of the True Parents, a small collection of pamphlets, booklets and her Divine Principle book. There was also a small box, neatly tucked away. Inside were a couple of hairs. She had found them on the sheets of the bed the True Parents had slept in. She treated this as if it were precious jewelry.

Fundraising through the sale of various items was how we made money to support the center. The basement was our assembly area for making products to sell. One of the first things I learned was how to make and sell "grainariums." We took glass-lidded jars of various sizes and filling them part way with different colors of grains, in layers, creating a design. We assembled dried flower arrangements, then placed them carefully into the jar of layered grains, then taped the lids shut. We would load the van up with boxes of grainariums and drive to an apartment complex or sometimes just a neighborhood where the houses were close together. We would then go door to door carrying a box with assorted colors and sizes of these creations, asking people to buy them to help our non-denominational church. I usually did pretty well at selling them. I think it was because I was so enthusiastic and excited about what I was doing.

We were taught to say as little as possible about what the money went for. That way, Satan couldn't invade and distract us from our mission to bring in money for God's work. We would simply say we were a non-denominational Christian youth group trying to help keep kids off drugs. It was exciting to know that one day those people who bought the grainariums or flowers from us would realize they had helped support the work of the Messiah. They would be the pride of their entire lineage one day. We just had to be trickier than Satan and stay focused on the mission at hand. God always had a plan and he always worked through the leaders in the church. I didn't have to worry about anything except doing what the leaders told me to do.

Another important activity was "witnessing," trying to get potential members to come to the center for a free dinner and to hear a lecture. We usually went to college campus areas to seek out potential members, mostly the University of Nebraska and Creighton University. The older members taught me how to witness. I worked with one of them at first, and then when I felt ready I would go talk with people by myself.

A technique that worked well was using a survey. I would stop someone or go sit next to him or her, if they were sitting alone, and ask them if they would be willing to take a survey. The survey started with their name and age and what they were studying in school. Then I would ask what their idea of the ideal world was. Before long we were discussing utopia and what the ideal world should be like, the same kinds of things I talked with members about during the walk to Des Moines. Eventually, I would tell them I thought they were special and invite them to dinner. I was really good at getting people to come for dinner, but not so good at screening them. Most of the time, the people I brought home were either there because they were interested in dating me or for the free dinner.

There was never personal time; there was too much work to do, and the house was always full of activity. Since bringing in new members was our most important mission, the main floor of the house was set up for bringing guests to dinner and lectures. There were posters on most of the walls promoting the group. Some had pictures of Moon and were from his speaking tours; others promoted the One World Crusade, which was a branch of the organization set up to create a movement for change, based on Moon's teachings. It was an evangelical group and consisted of mobile units that would witness and sponsor activities throughout the country to support the state centers.

Inside the front door stood a table full of literature, along with a guest book to sign. The dining room had a big table with plenty of room for members and guests to sit around for dinner. The living room was our lecture room. Folding chairs were set up in rows and there was a chalkboard in the front. Lectures went on several times a week. Whoever brought a guest would sit through the lecture with the guest. Other members would either cook or be working on tasks like preparing new grainariums for the next day of fundraising.

When guests came over we would make sure they were never without a member at their side, just like when I had been at the house the first time and during the walk. I understood now why it was so important. Satan would try to invade if we gave him the slightest opening. We tried to convince guests to come for a "retreat" at a regional center just for that purpose, where they would hear the entire lecture series. The retreat center was a small building in Iowa that had been a Grange hall at one time. The Iowa family had purchased it and invited the Nebraska center to join them for weekend retreats with potential members. Our goal with dinner guests was to convince them to come for the weekend. I usually stayed behind to fundraise, instead of going on the retreats.

For the most part, during my first few months, I either fundraised or witnessed. I began to learn the songs and absorb the way of life. I was proud of how successful at fundraising I consistently was. For some reason, people found it hard to say no to my insistence that they should buy a grainarium. Lokesh was always really enthusiastic about how well I did, which made me want to do even better. We worked long days and I was always glad to go upstairs to get some sleep at the end of the day, after our evening prayer session.

CHAPTER 4

THE TIMES
THEY ARE A' CHANGIN'
Bob Dylan

S EVERAL MONTHS AFTER I JOINED, we got word that there was
to be a fast and prayer on the steps of the Capitol Building
in Washington, D.C. We would be praying for Nixon not to be
impeached. I didn't understand the politics of the organization at
that point. The only thing I knew about the church and its politics
was what I heard shortly after I joined. When I told Lokesh about
the newspaper I originally planned to write for, thinking I could
still write the article to promote God's work, I told him that its
editor thought Moon was a fascist. Lokesh warned me to never
go back there. He said that Satan would try to stop me from doing
God's work. All those anti-war songs I had loved and the fact that
I used to call Nixon Tricky Dicky, blaming him for the war, didn't
matter anymore. I just knew that God had a plan that I would
someday understand.

The message was that we were to go to Washington immediately, so we loaded up the vans that very day and headed for
the Capitol. I had never been there. This was also my first chance
to meet members in a large gathering from all over the country,
even from different parts of the world. I loved the feeling of urgency and the immediacy of our response. We were rebuilding the
world. All governments had to be realigned with God's intentions.

We drove up to the steps of the Capitol building. Lokesh got
out and found someone who could tell us what we should do. He

came back wearing a sandwich board and pointed to where we could go get our own, then joined the group on the steps. The front of the board read, "I'm praying for…" and had the name of a congressman or senator and their picture. The back side had a quote from one of Moon's speeches with the heading, "In God We Trust."

We sat on those steps for three days and nights, sleeping on the steps at night using sleeping bags we had brought with us from Nebraska to keep us warm. Union Station became our bathroom and the place to brush our teeth.

I knew I was part of something far bigger than I could comprehend when I heard that Moon had met with Nixon earlier that week. We were on the cover of magazines and newspapers throughout the world. Still, it seemed strange to be praying for Nixon after being so strongly against him before I joined the church.

On the first afternoon we were there, I confessed to a brother who was sitting near me about how it felt for me, to be supporting Nixon. He hadn't been a member long and had a similar feeling of uneasiness. We talked for awhile about it, but kept coming back to the simple solution to our feelings of conflict: God had a plan that we couldn't possibly understand.

There was a speaker system set up and various church leaders talked to us throughout the days. Members would also sing songs, sometimes performing, sometimes leading us all in song. These were my new rock stars. I was proud when Dwight got up and played a song for everyone at one point. Neil Salonen, the president of the American Unification Church, spoke several times. Sometimes a congressman or senator would come out to meet the person who was praying for him.

The next day, I sat next to a sister named Carla, who had been in the church for several years. She was really friendly and very pretty. She had big brown eyes and full lips that turned a little sideways when she smiled. Carla treated me like I truly was her little sister. It was comforting. Growing up, I always wished I had an older sister. Instead, I had three older brothers, and two of them were so much older that I hardly knew them. She explained to me about the evils of Communism and how Father's plan was to end all war once and for all by aligning himself with world leaders who were opposed to communistic views, leaders like Nixon. I was sure she knew more than I about politics, and I believed everything she said.

Sitting on those steps with my True Family, I was relieved to know that I would never have to go to college or take some stupid meaningless job, such as working in a department store like my old roommate, Sharon. What I was doing made me someone who was on the front line of helping put an end to war and suffering.

After the three days, one of the church leaders announced that Father had invited us all to Belvedere, one of Moon's properties, a 35-acre estate on the Hudson River, where he lived. What was even more exciting was that Father would be speaking to us and everyone, of course, was very excited.

We drove to upstate New York and arrived at Moon's home, an estate like a big park, immaculately groomed. There was a pond filled with Koi fish on the property. They were big fish with bold colors. Some were white with bright orange blotches; others were black with bright yellow markings. I especially liked the ones that were white and red and black. I was told that when Father walked by the pond, the fish followed him.

Our group, the Nebraska family, ran and pushed our way to the front of where Moon would be speaking. There were several hundred members there that day. My little group wanted to be as close as we could get to where Father would be speaking. It reminded me of concerts I went to before I joined, with open seating; but here we didn't have to be so aggressive to get to the front. Crystal was especially excited. Her childlike attitude and Lokesh's continuous effort to offer her as an example of how a child of True Parents should behave gave us all permission to follow her lead, even though as I looked around it appeared that some members didn't appreciate our pushing through the crowd.

Lokesh was proud of our unapologetic desire to be as close to Father as we could get. I began to see a difference between the

Nebraska family and other branches of the family. Lokesh set the standards for devotion, hard work and enthusiasm extremely high, and I felt a sense of competitiveness when we were around non-Nebraska family members. I was proud to be in Lokesh's group and kept looking at him, studying his every move, his smile, the way he bowed his head to pray, his unquestionable devotion to Father and Mother.

When I saw the face of my Messiah, I felt lightheaded. Then, he glanced in my direction and it seemed as if our eyes met. He smiled, and I began to cry. What he said didn't matter very much to me. I felt like I was in one of those pictures in the books from my Sunday school classes of Jesus talking to a group of children. Moon talked through an interpreter for quite a while. I tried to take in what he was saying. He talked about God's dispensation —a phrase that was used a lot when talking about God's plan—and how the world would soon understand the Divine Principle. I looked around for some of the brothers and sisters I had met during those days on the steps, especially the sister who told me about Communism, but never had the chance to talk with any of them again.

After the talk everyone received Big Macs for lunch because it was one of Father's favorite things to eat. I never liked Big Macs. The "special sauce" was gross to me, but I got it down. We sat in a circle on the lawn and talked about what Father had said. Lokesh informed us that we would be heading back to Nebraska right away. God's work was waiting for us.

Shortly after eating, we got in our vans and headed for home, a 20-hour drive. I drove part of the way, even though I had a total of about four hours' driving experience prior to that trip. I had my license, but had only driven around York on a couple of occasions with my mom. I was nervous, but Dwight sat next to me and was patient with my lack of experience. He helped me remember basic things, like slowing down before it was time to get off at an exit. "I forget you are so young," he said, giving me a brotherly teasing wink.

Back home, I felt an even deeper dedication. Seeing Father's estate and how involved we were with politics made me realize how quickly we would take over the world and implement God's plan to rebuild everything according to His divine plan.

I wanted to win Lokesh's respect. Crystal treated Lokesh with a similar adoration as she did the True Parents, and her behavior was a model for everyone in the Nebraska family. Lokesh made sure we understood that. She would scramble for crumbs he dropped—literally. If he left a bit of food on his plate, she would eat it when he was through, as if it were holy. The doctrine clearly supported hierarchy, but this took it to a new level. I couldn't compete with that puppy-like behavior. It just wasn't me, and I knew it would come off as fake for me to act like she did.

It was obvious that Crystal had a special relationship with Lokesh, which I longed for. During the following months, I fasted several times. I did an eight-day fast with no food or water. I dried out. My lips were chapped. I held wet washcloths up to them and couldn't wait to brush my teeth, wanting so much to let some of the water in my mouth down my throat, but never swallowed. It was winter, fortunately. Had it been hot, it would have been extremely dangerous. I could have died. No one ever told me there was anything wrong with it. I just wanted to prove my dedication. I was dizzy and toward the end, everything was confusing. My tongue felt swollen.

Later I did a 21-day fast, but this time with water. It was difficult to fundraise during that time. I became very weak. I was cold, even when I was wrapped up in a blanket or wearing a coat, and began to shake during my last week. Jake seemed irritated with me for not being stronger. He didn't seem impressed with my dedication—just irritated that I wasn't able to produce more. Like in the previous fast, I became dizzy and confused. I had an important "revelation," though, toward the end of the fast, and realized what my ultimate mission was.

I had heard a speech of Moon's that talked about how every being, both alive and in the spirit world, would eventually be allowed into the Kingdom of Heaven, when all indemnity was paid. According to the speech, even Satan would eventually be allowed to enter. He would be Lucifer again, a restored angel. That speech was part of a morning reading during one of the last few days of my fast. I walked around the center that day in a daze. On the 20th day of my fast I could hardly walk. Dwight looked at me as they were eating their breakfast and told me to stay home and do laundry instead of fundraising. Just carrying clothes to the washer was exhausting. I kept imagining Satan entering the Kingdom of Heaven one day. I kept thinking about the fact that Satan, being the furthest from God, would be the last to enter the Kingdom of Heaven.

Someone had to be his spiritual parent, and I began to wonder who that would be. I knew that whoever it was would have to develop the kind of heart that could forgive the cause of all pain and all evil that has ever existed. While folding clothes, and delusional from fasting, I decided that I was the woman for the job.

I knew it would be a hard course, but I believed it was my mission. I decided I should always volunteer for the most difficult or lowly tasks. This would be how I would prepare myself for having the kind of heart that could love and forgive Satan. The more indemnity I paid the better. I would be the one who would finally close the door to hell forever.

A few months later when Christmas was coming, I felt Satan at work. My Mom had called several times, wanting me to come to their house for Christmas day. I was living at the Lincoln Center at the time, spending everyday fundraising. We were working really hard because money was not coming in as fast as we needed. I didn't really like being in Lincoln; Lokesh was in Omaha, and the Center there was nicer. And it felt strange not to celebrate Christmas. I felt sorry for myself, and prayed hard to make the feeling go away. I knew it was Satan trying to tear down my commitment.

On Christmas evening, unannounced, my family showed up at the Lincoln Center. We were completely unprepared for them. It was awkward for everyone, but my family—the one I grew up with, my blood family—didn't seem to mind the awkwardness as much as we did.

They didn't stay long, but they had brought presents for me. So Crystal took me aside and told me I could give them each

grainariums, which I did. Immediately I felt guilty from both direc-
tions. I knew how much the Nebraska family was struggling financially and what that many grainariums represented in sales. I also
knew that my family didn't really appreciate them and would have
preferred I had come to my parents' house and brought presents that
meant I had thought about each of them. I was glad when they left.

That night as I prayed before going to sleep, I couldn't stop
crying. No one heard me; the sisters were already asleep. I thought
of the story we had been told about Father when God revealed the
Divine Principle to him. We were told that when he understood
God's suffering heart, he cried so long and hard that tears came
through the floor to the room below him. I fell asleep clutching
my picture of the True Parents.

Satan continued to work on my family. My brother Bryce got
married to his high school sweetheart, Sal, during my first year in
the Church. I was very upset. I wanted Bryce to have True Father
choose his mate. Now that the Messiah was on the earth, he could
pick mates for everyone and bless their marriages. That way their
children would be born free of the original sin, free of Satan's
blood lineage. The thought that Bryce would have children with
the blood of Satan in them was horrible. I loved him and knew
his children would suffer unnecessarily with sin.

It made me really sad to think that Bryce, along with the
rest of my family, would think this meaningless ceremony gave
him and Sal permission to have sex and even bear children. This
would be a day of great sadness for God. I must have not worked
hard enough or sacrificed enough for this tragedy to happen.

I was supposed to be in the wedding. I showed up late with
Maggie and Beth, two of the sisters from Omaha. We were all
dressed in conservative, out of style clothes that were from a sec-
ondhand store. I knew we stood out, and I was proud and full of
righteousness about it.

My younger sister, Julie, had filled in for me as bridesmaid.
I felt no connection with her at all. I hadn't for years, though.
I knew she had been mad at me for not being more normal. I
had been causing turmoil in the family from the time I started

skipping school and getting in trouble as a teenager. The day of our brother's wedding, she didn't speak to me.

I cried at the wedding, but mine were tears of righteousness for what a mistake they were making. As we left, I stopped to ask the minister who had performed the wedding if he really thought it had been a God-centered wedding. He said, "I certainly hope so," with a big smile. He had no idea what harm he had just done. I felt frustrated that the news of the Messiah being on earth was taking so long to spread.

I left without going to the reception or even talking with Bryce or any of my family, except my Mom, who seemed upset and worried. She wanted me to stay, but I had to go.

As the months went by, I visited my parents and Julie a few times. Julie still lived at home; she was three years younger than me, fourteen at the time. I always had Family members with me when I visited. The goal was to try to help them get through the barrier Satan had built between them and the Divine Principle.

One time Crystal and I decided to make Korean food for them. Crystal had learned to prepare it when Father came to Omaha on his speaking tour. She was really proud of that and thought it would be a great *condition* for my family to eat food from the Fatherland. (Condition was a term we used often. All of history, according to Moon's teachings, was based on conditional situations that could allow God to work. It was like a strategic competition between God and Satan with specific rules.) Crystal made a beef dish called bulgogee and a spicy cabbage dish called kimchee. I could tell they didn't like it very much. Julie wouldn't even try the kimchee. After dinner, we sat in the living room and Crystal decided to sing a song. She broke into Karen Carpenter's "I Won't Last a Day Without You." Julie couldn't take it. She left the room with disgust on her face. I watched her leave, knowing I wasn't the cool big sister she wanted me to be. One day she would understand, though, and would thank me for what I was doing. We left a mess in the kitchen that many years later Julie still resented having to clean up, and headed back to Omaha.

CHAPTER 5

FATHER AND SON
Cat Stevens

I PRAYED EVERY DAY for my family to join the True Family and felt my prayers were being answered when I learned that my Mom and Dad were going on a vacation to Hawaii at the same time Moon would be speaking there. I was sure this was God's work.

Their best friends, Wally and Bernice, whom I had known most of my life, were going there, compliments of the car dealership for which Wally worked, and they invited my parents to come along. When I told Lokesh about it he got excited and agreed that it must be God working. He said that I should go and take my parents to hear Father speak. He made it very clear that it was really important that my Mom and Dad agree to attend Moon's speech. Lokesh wanted my Dad to pay for my trip, but Dad said he couldn't afford it.

It was a lot of money for the ticket and I was really discouraged that I wasn't going to get to go, but at the last minute I got great news. I was going. Lokesh somehow pulled the money together.

"I prayed about this," he told me. "You have been working really hard for the True Parents and I really feel God wants your family to attend this, so I bought you a ticket." He went on to say that I would still need to get money from my parents for expenses.

He explained that if they gave me money, it would set a good condition for God to work. Lokesh made arrangements with the Hawaii church director for me to stay at the local center.

I was on the same plane as my parents and Wally and Bernice. While on the plane, I found out that the big banquet for the car dealers was happening on the same night as Moon's speech. I knew it was Satan at work and had to find a way to get them to come. By the end of the plane ride my Mom said she would try to come, at least for a while. Dad was definitely not coming. I couldn't bring myself to ask for money.

When we arrived in Hawaii I said goodbye to my parents and Wally and Bernice and told them I would talk with them later. I told them someone was coming to pick me up. When I called the phone number for the center, nobody answered. I hitchhiked to the address on the piece of paper Lokesh had given me. Someone picked me up but was only going part way, so I ended up walking a couple miles, but I didn't mind. Everywhere I looked it was so beautiful and so different from anything I had ever seen. The smells were sweet and reminded me of powder I had smelled in my Aunt Grace's bedroom. The colors of the flowers were so vibrant I repeatedly stopped to stare at them. In Nebraska there are flowers, but these were completely different. Sometimes on one single bloom there was bright blue and bright yellow with shades of purple and pink. Some of them looked like they were made of wax. I had to touch them to know for sure they were real.

When I finally found the address of the center and rang the doorbell, the person who answered seemed confused. She obviously didn't know I was coming, but she asked me to come in and then went to find the center director. He wasn't there. I was relieved when a Japanese sister finally greeted me with welcoming acknowledgment. She had at least heard about me. Unfortunately, she was on her way out the door, but she told me to make myself at home. Everyone was frantically busy, preparing for the speech and for Father's arrival.

I didn't want to get in the way and didn't know what I could do to help. Some of the sisters were talking about what they would be wearing to the speech. I decided to go back to the hotel where my parents were staying and ask my Mom if I could borrow something nicer than what I had brought to wear. Besides,

I needed to work on convincing them to come to the speech. Dad wasn't there. Mom agreed to loan me her brand new green pantsuit. I begged her to come to the speech. Finally she said she would come for a little while, but needed to get back to the banquet to be with Dad as early as possible. She told me that he definitely wasn't going to come, since Wally's big banquet would be going on. I decided to stay near the hotel for the few hours I had until it was time to go to the speech. I walked around and sat near the ocean, praying. I dozed off in the sun for a time, then went back to the hotel and got ready to go.

Dad left for the banquet and Mom came with me to the speech. It was a small gathering, between 75 and 100 people. It started late and seemed to go on forever. I kept watching my Mom look at the clock. One of the reasons the speech took so long was that everything Moon said was in Korean and had to be translated. After the speech, Moon stood in a greeting line and shook hands with attendees. I insisted that we stay and shake his hand. She reluctantly agreed. I couldn't believe that my Mom was shaking the hand of the Messiah. I wanted so much for her to understand, but she didn't. I felt disappointed and discouraged.

After the handshake, she quickly and anxiously left to go meet up with my Dad. I stayed and got a ride back to the center with a member. The next day I called and talked to Mom. She told me that the car dealer's banquet was almost over by the time she got there and that my Dad was really irritated with her for going to Moon's speech. When I asked her what she thought of the speech, she told me that she didn't see anything special about Moon or his speech.

I had failed.

My flight left the next day. They would be staying another five days. Mom asked me to bring her pantsuit back to the hotel. She was planning on wearing it while she was there. I wanted to bring it to her but I didn't have enough time before I had to go.

I had to hitchhike to the airport. The Hawaii members left the house early the day I was leaving. They assumed I would be taking a cab to the airport and even gave me the phone number to call. They didn't realize I had no money and Lokesh was under the impression I was going to get what I needed from my Dad. I just thought I would figure out how to get by without it. I assumed God would take care of me.

Lokesh also assumed I would be taking a taxi home from the airport, again thanks to my Dad's help. I didn't want to tell him differently. I kept thinking about him telling me I had been doing good work for God, so I wanted to hide my failures from him.

The flight was delayed and I arrived in Omaha in the middle of the night. I asked the person sitting next to me on the plane if she was going near where I needed to go. She wasn't going my way, but offered me a ride to the bus station downtown. That seemed like a good idea.

CHAPTER 6

AMAZING GRACE
Various Artists

I STOOD IN THE BUS STATION with my bag in my hand, looking around for whom to approach for money to pay for a taxi. It was 3:00 in the morning. I approached a guy whose eyes met mine as I searched the room.

"Where do you need to go?" I gave him the address. "Wait here a minute, my friend has a car." Some time passed and he came back. "Out here." He led me to a car. I was happy that God had provided a ride for me.

It was a beat-up blue sedan and the driver was a big guy with dirty hair. The guy who had offered me the ride opened the back door for me. He took my bag from my hand and threw it into the front seat. I got in the back and a third guy, who seemed to come from nowhere, opened the other back door and got in. He had long stringy blond hair and smelled of body odor and stale alcohol. The guy who had offered me the ride got in beside me. I felt a little nervous, but just wanted to get to the house and sleep.

"Thanks so much for the ride." I gave the driver the address. No one said anything as we drove off. I tried to start a conversation, but the guy next to me kept rubbing my leg and nobody would talk to me. I felt the pressure of two bodies pushing on me from either side. I wanted to move away from the blond guy, but didn't want to get any closer to the one on my other side. I noticed we were going the wrong way and told the driver.

"I know where I'm going," he said. The blond guy was trying to kiss me. I kept trying to talk about being a missionary. It was still dark out and the lights of the city were growing dimmer as we kept driving further away from the address I had given him. We turned down a bumpy road and the car came to a stop near the gate of a landfill.

"Why are we here?" The blond guy opened the car door and pulled me out of the car. I began to pray for them. I knew that if they hurt me their indemnity would be terrible.

The driver started to pull me toward the gate that led into the dump. "I work for God, please, just let me go," I pleaded.

A fist struck me in my face. I thought that my being a good person would always protect me, yet blood was dripping from my nose and I was being forced further into the dump, further away from my bag that held the green jumpsuit my Mom had loaned me, my Bible, my copy of the Divine Principle. The smell of garbage was strong. It seemed useless to try to resist their hands clenching my arms as they took me deeper into the filth.

We stopped behind the rusting remnants of a pile of metal. There was a hint of light in the sky. Fundamental laws of the Divine Principle raced through my mind and I clung to them as my only resource. I knew I was one of a very few people on the planet who knew these laws, and, because I was a disciple of the second coming of Christ, I could not allow certain things to happen. It would be better for me to die than to allow them to rape me.

Because sex was the source of the original sin that had caused 6,000 years of suffering for God and mankind, anyone who had been exposed to the Divine Principle had a critical responsibility. I knew that I was in a unique position to restore the fall of man by staying pure until Father chose a mate for me. Then I could become half of a blessed couple. My children could then be part of God's first true lineage, separate from Satan. I defined sex, in that moment, as vaginal penetration and decided I would be all right if I just didn't allow that to happen.

As they ripped off my clothes I screamed, "I've had surgery!" The blond from the backseat yanked my hair and pulled me to my knees. "It won't work! I'm sewn up inside from surgery." I said this with so much certainty that they actually believed me. Instead, the big guy from the front seat crammed his prick down my throat. I threw up. At the same time, the blond was raping me from behind. I convinced myself it didn't count as fornication because it wasn't vaginal. The third one, the one who had offered me the ride, was holding me down, but he looked scared.

The big guy wasn't done and took a turn in my ass, and then he hit me several times in the face and grabbed a brick. "I'm gonna finish her off." His eyes were intense and darting around at an unnatural speed.

The one who had initially offered me a ride hadn't taken a turn yet. "Wait," he said.

Words came from somewhere inside me with absolute confidence. "I won't tell anyone. There are people looking for me right now and people who saw me get in the car with you at the bus station. I'm sure the police have already been called. They will find you. You have to get out of here." The big guy kicked me. "I swear, I won't tell anyone. No one will ever know this happened. You can still get away." The brick was still in his hand.

"Put it down. She's right," said the guy who offered me the ride. "Besides, it's my turn." The brick dropped on the ground. "You guys go ahead, I want her alone." The blond guy and the big guy left. "Just jerk me off," the remaining one said, taking my hand and placing it on his penis. I did what he said.

"I'm sorry," he said, after he ejaculated. He sat there a minute, and then told me: "I want to see you again. What's your number?"

I heard a voice in the distance screaming at him to hurry. I felt like I was going to puke again. I made up a number and gave it to him. "I'll call you," he said quietly, like it was our little secret, as he was running toward the car. I sat there naked among the beat-up metal until I heard the car speed away.

The sky was starting to have the beginnings of morning in it. I found my clothes, torn, bloody and filthy. I put them on.

I have no idea how far I walked. I knocked on the door of the first house I came to. It was a little house, old and not at all well kept. An elderly woman in a bathrobe answered.

"Can you help me?" The door slammed shut. I walked away. A pick-up truck came down the road toward me. I waved and it passed me by. Then I heard it stop and back up. There was a woman driving the truck. She was dressed like she was going to work. She was wearing a freshly ironed blouse and slacks. Her hair was shoulder length and flipped up at the bottom. She looked like she was in her forties. "Do you need a ride?" Then she looked at me more closely. "Get in." She reached over and opened the door for me. I got in the truck. "What in God's name happened to you? Maybe I'd better take you to a hospital," she said.

"I just need a phone," I said. "I'll be okay." The sun was almost up. We drove to a factory just down the road, where she worked. She kept asking me what happened. I felt my body shaking and kept telling myself to be strong, for God. I could not find the words to respond to her. It was hard to hold back tears and I finally just shook my head and looked down when she spoke to me. She finally quit asking and I sat quietly. We arrived at her work, and with her insistence, we went inside. Another woman was there. She covered her mouth with her hand when she saw me. They wanted to call the police or take me to a hospital. I kept saying no. "I just need to call someone to come and get me."

I called Lokesh.

One of the women wiped the blood from my face and gave me some ice to put on it, where it was swollen. Finally, Lokesh came. When I saw his car, I ran out the door saying thank you on my way out. I knew the woman who had helped me would want to talk to Lokesh, but I got in the car and we drove away before she could get out the door. Lokesh drove out of the area, and then pulled over near a park to talk to me.

While we were driving he kept asking me if I was all right. I told him what had happened. When I told him I had run out of money and had to find a ride home, he didn't seem concerned about that detail, which was a relief for me. I didn't want him to know I hadn't asked my Dad for money.

As I told the story, I emphasized that they didn't go inside me. I didn't cry and spoke in a monotone without emotion. It was hard to tell where the pain from one part of my body ended and where the pain from another part started. I just hurt. But at the same time I felt numb and like my body wasn't part of me; it seemed more like baggage I wanted to throw away.

"Are you sure they didn't penetrate you?" he kept asking. I knew he was worried about my place in the building of the Kingdom of Heaven. Father had made it very clear that if anyone who had heard the Divine Principle fornicated, they would not be able to become a blessed couple and could not be part of beginning the new lineage of people.

Lokesh explained to me that the reason Satan had been able to invade me like this was because I had been so sinful before I joined the Family. It was indemnity.

Hearing that from him didn't surprise me. One day, shortly after joining the group, when Lokesh was talking with me about what my life was like before meeting the church, I had told him about using a lot of drugs. He had been more concerned about whether I was a virgin. I wasn't. He was surprised when I told him that, mostly because I was still so young. Disappointment and disgust were apparent in his face, but his voice remained kind. Still, I heard pity in his tone, as he explained that I would need to work hard to pay indemnity for being so much a part of Satan's world.

As he looked me over, checking out the cuts and making sure nothing was broken, he was certain this was indemnity. "You must pray deeply and repent for letting Satan invade." He took my hands in his. They were dirty and had blood crusted on them. "I'll talk to Father; maybe you can still be blessed." I remained silent. What if I wouldn't be blessed? I was damaged goods, hoping for salvation.

We drove to the Center and entered the back door. Lokesh took me upstairs into the room where he slept. I had never been in there, except for a quick peek. He told me I could stay there for a few days and that I should take a shower and should leave my clothes by the door. A sister would bring me some clean clothes to put on. He pointed to the shower.

That was the shower the True Parents used when they stayed at the Center during their tour before I had joined. The room they had slept in was next door. I knew what an honor it was to use that shower.

I finally cried as I was taking my shower. The water hurt my skin. Everything hurt, but I was in the shower God's son had been in and I was alive.

My clothes were burned. I stayed in Lokesh's room for several days. He came and talked with me several times during those days. I told him about Hawaii and how discouraged I felt. He helped me understand that it would take time and reminded me how strongly Satan works through the people we are closest to, like our family. He told me I should pray and read the Divine Principle for three days. Word eventually came from the regional director, who had talked to Father directly about me. Lokesh came in my room, sat down on the bed and told me the good news. I could still be blessed. He seemed as relieved as I was by the news.

It was weeks before I went outside the Center. There were bruises all over my body. The whites in my eyes were completely blood red and my front tooth had a small chip. I was never taken to the doctor, and the police were never notified. I built grainariums and helped with cooking and cleaning. The bruises changed from pink to blue/black to yellowish green. The whites in my eyes began to clear after about a week, but it took another week or so for them to be completely clear of the blood. Lokesh instructed me that if anyone outside the family saw me and asked what happened, I should say I was in a car accident.

My Mom kept calling, asking for me. Each time, she was told I was out. One day she showed up at the Omaha Center, unannounced. I heard her voice from behind the door where I hid from her sight. When she was told, yet again, that I was out, she asked for the green pantsuit. "I'll just go look for it myself," she said, and asked where the closet was. She was taken upstairs, but of course, it wasn't there.

CHAPTER 7

DON'T STOP
Fleetwood Mac

ONE NIGHT, about a year after I joined, when we came home from fundraising in an apartment complex, Lokesh told me he needed to talk with me. From time to time, he would check in with me and give me advice on how to do better at some aspect of my life in the center; I assumed that was what was going on.

We went into a little porch area off the lecture room, and as soon as we sat down, I could see in his eyes that something more important was behind this conversation. "I have some important news for you," he said. "Father has requested that each state send one person to join his special mobile fundraising teams, the MFT. I have prayed about it and decided you are the best choice for the mission." He put a hand on each of my shoulders, smiling like a proud father. "Come on, Diane; don't look so scared, this is great." I felt my face shifting into a smile. He responded with another smile.

I would be leaving in two days. I was proud, excited and scared. Mostly, though, I was excited. The idea of getting to travel and meet new members of the family sounded great to me. "How long will I be gone?" I asked, like a child going on an adventure.

"There's no way of knowing. It's up to Father," he answered. That was not what I expected to hear. The excitement left, and after searching his face for some clue as to what that meant, I suddenly felt like crying. He saw the change in my face and responded with kindness. His big brown eyes told me he understood and would miss me as well. He stood up and I followed his lead. He put an arm around my shoulder and we walked out to the lecture room.

Activity filled the house that night. We had several new members who were the focus of the more senior members' attention. The brothers unloaded partially filled boxes with unsold grainariums in them from the van. We would refill them with new product. We had a good night, so most of the boxes only had a few left in them. They could hold about nine per box. I had emptied my box.

Lokesh spent a few more minutes talking with me as we stood in the lecture room. He explained that Jake would be driving me to Chicago, where we would meet up with members from around the region. Those of us who were chosen for the mission would then drive together to New York. He told me that he would announce the news to everyone at evening service and asked me to go and gather everyone in preparation.

Dwight led the service that night. We all sat on the floor behind the chairs in the lecture room. Sisters were together on one side of the group, brothers on the other. Dwight and Lokesh faced us.

The service started, as always, with a prayer. Dwight then said that before the reading of Father's words, Lokesh had an announcement. This is when Lokesh told everyone of my new mission. Maggie was sitting next to me. I had never felt very close to her; she tended to keep to herself. But I had known her since the first day we met in the van driving to Omaha to begin the walk. She gave me a hug.

"You will all have time to say your goodbyes over the next two days," Lokesh told everyone, and turned the service back over to Dwight. Dwight read from *Master Speaks*, a book of speeches that had been given at different times by Sun Myung Moon. I had a hard time concentrating on the speech. There was a lump in my throat. The service seemed to drag on forever as we sang a holy song and then had a unison prayer. And then we sang still one more song before Dwight finally ended the service with a prayer.

In the prayer he asked Heavenly Father to watch over me on my new mission. I couldn't hold the tears back any longer. With the word "amen" spoken, everyone immediately surrounded me with their excitement, encouragement and hugs.

The next two days were a blur of deciding what to take in my one small suitcase and trying to spend whatever time I could with everyone before I had to say my final goodbyes. I felt close to several of the members, and others were like classmates in school that I sat next to all year, but hardly noticed.

When Lokesh first told me that Jake would be driving me to Chicago, to meet up with other members who were also beginning the new mission, I was disappointed. My feelings toward Jake had never grown deeper since I first met him on the walk. He reminded me a little of Herman Munster. He towered over everyone and had a similar haircut and bone structure; his grin was also similar to Herman's. His claim to fame was singing "Lord of La Mancha." He was a tenor, and he sang with such power that I always felt like the room shook a bit when he performed. Sometimes when he sang, bits of spit would fly from his mouth, and he always performed that song as if he were on a stage, arm gestures emphasizing the message that, "I am I, Don Quixote, the Lord of La Mancha."

Jake and I took turns driving and sleeping during the trip to Chicago. I preferred driving. It gave me time to think. I decided that for the first full day of travel, I would only reflect on where I was coming from. Later, I could look forward to what was in front of me. A Korean brother I had met when I was in D.C. praying for Nixon told me that in Korean culture, new beginnings in life were always started in that fashion to pay homage to the place one was leaving. Since Korea was the "Fatherland," I wanted to do everything I could to make their traditions mine. I knew I would also need to learn the Korean language, because it wouldn't be long before it became the universal language, once everyone knew who Father was.

My Mom and Dad would be upset when they found out I wouldn't come back to Nebraska for a while. I wanted to find out more about my mission before telling them any details, so when calling my Mom before we left, instead of the truth, I told her I was going to New York for a training and wasn't sure how long I would be gone. My goal was to work really hard to lay a foundation for God to work on the task of bringing them into the True Family. It might be a while before I would see them again. I thought about my Dad's dimples when he smiled and how he would call me "darlin."

I reminded myself about the Divine Principle and God's laws of indemnity. The world was created with laws. God created the laws and he has to follow them, even if it causes him tremendous pain to do so. If we, as his children, break those laws, then indemnity has to be paid so that we can return to our true nature. It had taken thousands of years for indemnity to be paid through the blood and sweat of our ancestors so that the Messiah could return. That was because Jesus's followers failed their mission.

I thought about how sad it made God to see his children suffer. He had no choice; he could not break his own laws. This explained all suffering. Suffering was the road home to God's Kingdom of Heaven. I was ready to suffer for my family. I knew God chose me to be his disciple and I would not let him down.

Jake was snoring in the passenger seat. I was glad he was sleeping. I didn't have any reason to dislike Jake. My emotions were just too close to the surface to try to relate to him. I felt much more intimate with my own thoughts than I would feel in robotic conversation with him. The snoring was comforting. My mind moved on to Lokesh and all the members of the Nebraska family. One by one, I thought of each member. I would miss Dwight's 12-string guitar and his upbeat way that always made me smile. But I knew I would miss Lokesh and Crystal the most.

When we arrived in Chicago, there was no time lost before we had to get on the road again. Jake shook my hand and told me everyone would be praying for me. We unloaded my things from one van into the other and were off.

There were three sisters and two brothers in the van heading to New York. The brothers were in the front. They took turns driving. We sang songs and told our stories as we drove. We each told our story of how we had joined and how long we had been a member as well as any experiences we had with the True Parents. I waited anxiously for my turn to tell my story. I told my story about the walk and being invited into the house by Father. I described sitting in front of Father and Mother and listening to him talk with our little group, then hearing Hyo Jin sing, all on the day after I joined. Everyone listened raptly. We slept that night leaning on each other's shoulders, only stopping for fast food and to use the bathroom.

Our destination was a property called Barrytown in upstate New York. When we pulled up to the entrance, it was like arriving at Oz. This was proof that I was part of something that was capable of changing the world. The property consisted of 250 acres and numerous buildings. There was no free time to explore; I just took it all in.

From the moment we got out of the van, someone was giving us direction as to what to do. I felt like a soldier arriving at boot camp. But, instead of defending a country, I was God's soldier. There was a peace that came with knowing that following was all I needed to do. I was certain someone closer to God was leading me where I needed to go. Nothing about my life and destiny was my responsibility. As I walked across the lawn, watching brothers and sisters I had never met coming in and out of the buildings, all looking like they were going somewhere with a purpose, I thought about how confused and frustrated I had been before joining, trying to figure out what to do with my life. I was struck by the relief I felt in knowing I was surrendering my free will to the True Parents. I looked around the property and promised God I would follow without question.

Tucked away in a drawer, I still have some photos of myself from my days in the group. Among them, there is one of me standing in Barrytown, on that first day. I was wearing a short-sleeved yellow floral dress that went just below my knees. It had a high neckline and the fit was not flattering. I looked a little pudgy after gaining back the weight lost from fasting, and then some.

I had short hair, just below the ears. Maggie had cut it for me in Nebraska. She did the best she could, but had very little experience, so it was a little uneven on one side and was held back with a barrette. There is a smile on my face, but my eyes lack presence, hinting at my exhaustion.

Before being assigned to our teams, we stayed at Barrytown for several days. A Japanese sister took a group of us to a big room set up like an army barracks. She assigned cots to each of us. It was better than the floor, I thought, sitting on my bed for a moment before continuing the tour.

The excitement I felt was reflected in most of the faces that surrounded me. When I saw traces of fear or fatigue in some of the members, I avoided them. I was on a cloud and refused to fall off. We ate breakfast in a cafeteria after a few hours of sleep and then quickly gathered in the auditorium, where we sat on the floor for lectures. Sisters sat on one side of an aisle and brothers on the other. Various leaders from the church spoke to us about how important our mission was.

One day Father showed up. He was wearing a wool cardigan sweater with a collar and black slacks. His interpreter once again at his side, he spoke with gentle casualness in the beginning about being happy to see us, and how happy it made God that we were here. His smile was tender and warm. He thanked us for our hard work and then talked at length about the importance of his current speaking tour in God's dispensation. We would be raising money for the tour. As he described the struggle between God and Satan, he became animated. His face filled with determined rage.

Suddenly, he began to ask us questions. "Do you understand how important your work is?" He would cup his hand to his ear after asking each question, insisting on our loud response. "What if you get tired?" As he asked this question, he would act as if he were falling asleep; we laughed. "Will you say, 'I'm too tired,' and go take a nap?" Again he cupped his hand by his ear.

"NO!!" we screamed.

"Maybe a brother will meet a cute girl while he is out fundraising." Now he pretended to be flirting with a girl. We laughed again. "Will you say, I can do God's work later and go have some coffee with her?"

"NO!!" the brothers yelled.

Father went on asking questions about how we would react to difficult situations that could arise. The fervor built with each question. He then ended with "Can God trust you to fulfill his will?"

Yelling so loud my vocal cords hurt, I screamed, tears welling in my eyes: "YES!!!"

"Let's pray," he said. As he prayed, I wept. God was counting on me.

I was standing outside by the driveway when Father's limousine left that afternoon. I didn't see him get in the car at the other side of the grounds, but could see him through the window waving as the car passed by. Several of us chased after the limo, waving back.

A Japanese leader by the name of Ken Sudo, who had been part of the Family since its early days, gave us a long lecture the next day. It was about the importance of understanding the significance of Cain/Abel relationships and what subject and object means.

Adam and Eve had three sons after "the fall." Mr. Sudo explained how God's laws worked in a very orderly way to restore what had been destroyed. The first two sons were in the position to restore the fall. Cain was representative of the first sin, when Eve had sex with the serpent. Abel represented the second sin, when Eve tempted Adam into having premature sex instead of waiting until God blessed them in marriage. Relatively speaking, Abel was less evil. So, God set up a situation that would allow Cain to behave in a way that would demonstrate a desire to reject evil desires and thus reverse the fall of man. When God accepted Abel's offering and rejected Cain's, Cain should have humbled himself and been able to come to God through his brother. This would have laid the foundation to restore the fall. Instead, Cain succumbed to his jealousy, just as the serpent had when he was jealous of Adam. Cain killed his brother, Abel; thus, many generations would suffer and have to pay great indemnity before another foundation could be set for the fall to be restored.

This dynamic played out on a regular basis in the lives of all human beings, but especially among God's chosen. Mr. Sudo warned us that Satan would try to invade while we were doing our mission. It would be important to recognize, he said, that the team leaders were in the position of Abel. God had chosen them and would work through them. There might be times where we thought we could do a better job than they could at leading the team—that was Satan invading our thinking. The only way to reach God was when Cain and Abel united and worked together. Both had a responsibility to find a way to work in a united manner.

Mr. Sudo spent hours lecturing about Subject and Object relationships. This came from Chapter One of the Divine Principle. It was part of the explanation of the Principles of Creation. The message was similar to the Cain and Abel lecture; the main idea was that all things in creation had a subject and object relationship. The subject was the initiator, the object was the responder. God was the Prime Subject, the Creator. Human beings were the subjects to all other forms of creation. Men were subject to women. All existence worked in hierarchy. Once again, the point was hammered in to follow the team leader's instructions without question.

I had heard we would be leaving soon, so I decided it was time to call my Mom and Dad. I asked to use a phone. A Japanese sister led me to the phone and talked to me about what I would say to my Mom. I liked this sister. Her name was Keiko. She smiled a lot and was very encouraging and excited about my new mission with the Mobile Fundraising Teams, the MFT. She told me it was hard for family to understand how important our mission is. She advised me to tell them I would write lots of letters.

My mom answered. She sounded happy but worried when she heard my voice. It had been over a week since I had called her. "I'm great," I told her. "I'm going to be traveling on a fundraising team." She asked me questions to which I didn't know the answers, like when I was coming home and where exactly I was going. Keiko was standing next to me. "I'll write you lots of letters," I told her. When I hung up the phone, I felt like crying; not because I would miss her, but because she didn't understand that the Messiah was here.

CHAPTER 8

MONEY
Pink Floyd

THE NEXT DAY WE WERE ASSIGNED to our teams and territories; I was going to Texas. My team Captain's name was Chris. He was tall with a medium build, probably in his 20s, and had a receding hairline. He seemed very serious and didn't say a lot. There was also a team mother assigned to the team, and she made up for his quietness. Her name was Toshiko and she was full of energy and enthusiasm. She was small but quite muscular, for a woman.

A group of Japanese members had come into the country to teach American members how to work harder and follow hierarchy better; Toshiko was one of them. When I met her, she was loading boxes into the van that we would be taking to our territory. There was a line of vans being loaded, all Dodges, all the same body type. They were big, with windows along the sides and three bench seats. Cargo was stored behind the seats. Our van was blue.

"Hi, hi," Toshiko said, shaking my hand and smiling. "I'm Toshiko-san. Want to help me?" I grabbed a box to pack in the back. I felt myself shifting into high gear to keep up with her.

"Careful. Easy to break," Toshiko commanded, still smiling, but without slowing down a beat. I moved quickly and carefully, following her pace and technique. The boxes were filled with butterflies, real butterflies and moths mounted on pieces of natural cork with dried flowers or foliage and encased in a rectangular Plexiglas box. A piece of paper was attached to the bottom of each one, providing the name of the particular butterfly or moth and where it was from. A team of Japanese sisters had assembled them, and they were beautiful.

We were on our way by early evening and would be driving all night. The van was stuffed to the ceiling with our bags, candy and butterflies. Part of the far back seat also had bags stuffed in, with just enough room for one person to sit. There were nine of us: Captain drove, Toshiko-san rode in the front passenger seat, two sisters and I sat in the first seat behind them and the four brothers sat in the back two rows.

We slept as we drove that night. Captain traded places with one of the brothers in the middle of the night so that he could get some sleep. The next day, we pulled into a grocery store and Toshiko went inside, returning with yogurt, apples, and donuts. As we ate and continued the drive, we took turns telling our "how we met the family" stories. I took my time telling my story, knowing the mileage it would give me. When Toshiko heard my story she explained that in Japan, most of the members—many of whom had been part of the church for years—had never seen the True Parents, except in pictures. Feeling I had climbed to the top of the pecking order, just below Toshiko, I adjusted my posture, sitting a bit taller the rest of the ride.

We arrived at our destination that evening and checked into a motel. We got two rooms, one for the brothers and one for the sisters. Captain told us to take showers and that he would be back with dinner. Toshiko talked with him before he left. I overheard her telling him to drive around and plan our drop-off points for the next morning, and also to get food for breakfast. She was very respectful of him, but seemed to be the one in charge. His eyes were bloodshot and looked like he could barely hold them open. His clothes were crumpled. I felt sorry for him, and knew I was going to like being on his team.

He was gone for a couple of hours and came back with buckets of chicken and a few bags of groceries. Toshiko took the groceries into the sisters' room. We gathered in the brothers' room to eat the chicken and have evening service.

The next morning Toshiko was up before anyone else. When I woke up, I saw her praying in front of a picture of Father.

Toshiko passed out powdered sugar donuts with orange juice for breakfast and we had morning service in the van on our way to our drop-off places. Mine was a busy avenue that had businesses lining both sides of the street. There were fast food restaurants, strip malls, gas stations and assorted other businesses. It went on for miles.

We pulled into a gas station. "This is your area, Diane," Captain announced. I hopped out with a case of Thin Mints and to ask if I could leave it there for a few hours. The guy working there said it would be fine. Captain then took me back down the street about a mile and told me to work my way to the gas station. "By then," he said in an upbeat tone, "you should be out of candy. You can get the new case from the gas station and keep going." He told me to watch my time so that I could cross the street and work my way back to the gas station to meet up with him. He would pick me up there in three hours.

"Do this for Father!" he said before he drove off. The candy was two dollars a box or three boxes for five dollars. There were 24 boxes in the case. I balanced the case on my hip and ran toward the door of a brake repair shop.

There were two men standing behind the counter and a few customers sitting waiting for their cars, reading magazines. I walked up to the younger guy, who was wearing a baseball cap and looking at some paperwork, sat my case down on the floor, grabbed three boxes out of it and handed them to him.

"Hi," I said before words could leave his open mouth. "Could you buy some candy to help keep kids off drugs?" He looked at the boxes of candy in his hands. "They're really good and it really helps." The older man, also behind the counter, and the customer he was assisting were both watching us, peripherally, as they continued their conversation. The younger guy caught the glance of the older man, and without words asked what he should do.

"How much?" the older man asked.

"Three for five dollars." I hesitated for a moment, and then broke the silence. "You can get one for two dollars but three is a

better deal and it really helps the kids. I'm with a non-denominational church."

"Take five bucks out of petty cash," he told the guy with the
baseball cap. The young man smiled at me, and then went to get
the money. As I was saying thank you, a woman who was looking
at a magazine while sitting next to the popcorn maker said she
would take one, too.

No one else was interested, so I headed for the next place,
which was a convenience store. The woman in there was less
friendly. When I approached a customer as I was coming in the
door, she yelled: "Hey, no soliciting."

"Sorry," I said and went on to the next place. I prayed for both
of them as I walked to the next business, knowing this would probably be the closest they would ever get to helping the Messiah.

By the time I got to the gas station, I had sold most of my
case. I took the remaining four boxes and rearranged the new case
so that I could fit the four boxes in. Balancing the new case on my
hip, I continued, checking the time. I had about an hour before
Captain would pick me up. My goal was to sell all my candy before
I was picked up.

My bag, which was chosen specifically for its long strap and
zipper closure, was slung over my head. I stuffed dollars into it as I
sold my candy. A growing wad of bills began to fill it and cushion
my stress. There wasn't much more time before I would be picked
up, and the results of my efforts would be measured by those bills.
I looked at my watch. There were a few more businesses up ahead;
I could still reach them before heading back to the gas station.

The donut shop was bustling and seemed like a good place to
sell a few more boxes of mints. The first person I approached was
a woman who wanted to talk with me about the Bible. She asked
me lots of questions I wasn't sure how to answer. I just wanted
to go. I felt like it was Satan invading and with every minute that
passed I felt worse.

"Sorry," I finally said, "but I have to go." I left the shop with
the half case of candy weighing heavily on my hip. I felt like crying. I knew better than to let Satan invade my mission.

When the van pulled up, I felt like a failure. Captain jumped out and ran around to the back to load my remaining candy. "Is this all?" he asked, taking my box.

"Yes," I replied, with a hint of renewed hope that maybe I hadn't let God down too terribly.

He put the box in the back and closed the door. "Excellent," he said, much to my relief and surprise.

When I got into the van, a brother named Tim was in the passenger seat and one of the sisters was in the seat directly behind him. Toshiko was in the next seat making sandwiches.

"Please pray," Captain said when I sat down. I bent over, resting my forehead on my clasped hands. Despite Captain's positive feedback, I prayed for forgiveness for losing concentration on my mission and for not selling out. When I finished and looked up, Toshiko handed me a peanut butter, banana and granola sandwich. We were pulling into a busy grocery store parking lot.

"Okay," Captain said. "I'm going to leave you here for about an hour. You're doing great." He told me to work the parking lot. "Just run up to people as they are getting into their cars. Try not to get too close to the entrance, so the manager doesn't kick you out."

He left me with a full case of candy and drove off. I took my sandwich with me and finished my lunch, leaning against a tree, my case of candy next to me. The sandwich was delicious. Toshiko had handed me a paper cup filled with orange juice just before they left. I finished it in one tip of the cup, washing down the peanut butter still stuck in my throat.

I sold half my case before pick-up.

After the parking lot, Captain drove me to my new area. It was all industrial and I had an hour. Again I sold about half a case. It was 5:30 when the van pulled up; I could hear singing as it approached.

I got in and sat on the bench seat behind the front seats with two other sisters, Angela and Molly. Angela was tall and skinny and had a long face. She had blonde hair and wore glasses. She was probably in her early 20s. Molly had dark hair. She wore it pulled back with a hair band. She had olive skin and was slightly pudgy. She smiled easily and patted my leg when I sat down next to her. I immediately bowed my head to pray as the singing continued.

The van was stopping when I lifted my head. There were two brothers with their cases of candy in their arms waiting by a bus stop. Captain hurried around to the back of the van and the brothers got in and joined Charlie, who had been sitting in the back seat by himself. Kevin started to talk as he was sitting down, but Captain stopped him and reminded them both to pray first.

We drove through a McDonalds and ordered food for our dinner, then drove to a park, counting our money on the way. There was a bucket for us to dump our change into after counting it. Toshiko instructed us how to straighten out the dollars and have all the faces the same way, then put them in rubber bands and pass the bundle to her. She put the bundles into a bank bag. She wrote down our totals. I had the largest total: $128. One brother, Kevin, had made less than $30.

We sat in a circle in the park, ate our burgers and fries and drank our cokes, and debriefed our day—how there were times we knew God was working, and how Satan had invaded at other times.

After we had finished eating dinner, Captain pulled into an apartment complex. This time our product was butterflies.

I was excited about selling the butterflies. They were so unique and beautiful. We worked opposite sides of the apartment complex and met up again at the same place we started for pick-up. Almost everyone thought the butterflies were beautiful, but the apartments were low income and a lot of the people said they just didn't have the money right now. I did sell a few, though. One young woman who came to the door told me she thought it was gross when I told her they were real and practically slammed the door in my face.

Another woman had me come in and take each one out. The Blue Morpho from Peru seemed to be everyone's favorite; its six-inch wingspan shimmered with an iridescent blue. Some of the giant moths, like the Sunset Moth from Madagascar, were spectacular as well. All of them were beautiful. She held each one up to the light to see the variations of color. I was anxious about taking so much time with one person and was relieved when she finally made her choice and paid me. She eventually settled on the Blue Morpho, which cost $15.

It was starting to get dark when the van arrived. Captain was about half an hour late. Kevin and I waited at our pick-up location. He talked to me the whole time. He told me he had joined with his brother and that his brother was on another team that went to Idaho. He was the younger of the two.

Kevin's tie was messy and his shirt was wrinkled. He seemed nervous all the time, fidgeting with his watch and scratching his head. He hadn't sold a single butterfly, but didn't seem to feel bad about it. I was glad when the van finally showed up.

"Sorry we're late," Captain said without explanation. We got in and prayed.

It was time to blitz the bars. Armed with a case of Thin Mints, I looked around at the area I would be working as the van drove away. There were three bars within walking distance. "I'll be back in about 20 minutes," Captain said, confident and moving like a runner who had hit his stride. I picked up on his energy and was ready to jump into action. Kevin was with me again. He was supposed to go to the big bar; I was to go to the two smaller ones.

Inside the first of my bars, the music was loud and the smell of cigarettes thick. I walked in like I had been a regular for years. Heading to the back of the room, I kneeled down next to some old drunk guy with a cowboy hat on. He put his arm around me when I asked him if he would buy some candy. "I'll buy some candy if you let me buy you a beer," he said.

"Stop harassing that girl and buy me some candy," a woman with big hair told him. She winked at me as she sucked on her cigarette, and then leaned her head back, blowing the smoke in the air and tapping the ashes in the ashtray filled with smashed butts stained with red lipstick. "Don't mind him," she said.

He bought some mints, and I moved on to the next table. By the time I was done, my twenty minutes were used up. I smelled like an ashtray.

Kevin hadn't made it past the bouncer at his bar. He had gone to the other little bar I was supposed to go to, but hadn't had time for, looking for me. He sold a few boxes there.

When we had worked our way through every bar in town, we finally headed for our motel room. I was fending off sleep spirits on the way to the motel while Toshiko read some of Fathers' words. Sleep spirits were a common problem among family members; satanic spirits would pull at our eyelids, trying to make us want to go to sleep. We talked about them often and prayed for them to leave us alone. We finished our evening prayer session as we pulled into the motel parking lot.

When we got in the room, some of the sisters decided to take showers. I said I would take mine in the morning and volunteered to sleep on the floor. I immediately fell asleep while inside my sleeping bag, kneeling for my nighttime prayer.

Captain knocked on our door early the next morning. It was time to do it again. Within a few days, we had done all we could in Amarillo and headed for Lubbock.

I was consistently one of the top sellers on the team. The weeks passed, becoming months. We worked our way through small cities and a couple of smaller towns. Dallas and Houston had teams dedicated to them, but I felt at home in small towns. Some days, I would get dropped off and have the whole town to myself. Captain would come and get me at five or six in the evening. I would work my way through all the businesses and then start knocking on doors in neighborhoods.

We were allowed to spend a few dollars on food when there wasn't something made for us ahead of time. Toshiko left the team to go work with another team after a couple of months, and, after she left, we almost always ate fast food. When someone needed a pair of shoes or clothes, we went to K-mart. We were very careful about spending God's money.

Our product changed from boxes of Thin Mints to big pieces of gum. The package the gum came in made it look like one huge stick of gum the size of a bumper sticker. There were three flavors: Black Jack, Clove and Beemans. The big slab of gum inside had perforations so you could rip off a normal-sized stick once you opened the package. We sold them for a dollar a piece or three for two dollars. This meant an easier sale than the boxes of candy we usually sold, but it took a lot more sales to make the same amount of money.

One day I got dropped off at a rodeo with several boxes of gum. My typical sales' line was that we were a Christian youth group raising money to keep kids off drugs. Between the cool product and the good cause, I was a hit. I stopped everyone that passed by me and asked them to buy some gum. Pretty soon people were trying to find me. "Hey, are you the girl selling gum for your church?"

We had a catch phrase for lying in this way: we called it "heavenly deception." The justification was that anyone who donated money to the cause of the Messiah would be blessed beyond measure. On the other side, Satan was constantly working through the media and through every person's innate "satanic nature" to prevent them from giving to the Messiah. It was our responsibility to do whatever was necessary to allow the people we met to receive the blessing of making a donation to the True Parents. In my mind this wasn't a stretch. It was keeping me, and a lot of young people like me, off drugs.

I sold out of my gum in just a few hours, even though I had taken far more than I thought I could sell. That day, I broke $300 for the first time. It was shameful to make under $100 in a day, but $300 was something that rarely happened. As I watched the cowboys drinking beer and spitting tobacco, I knew they had a lot of sin to pay for, and I was giving them that chance. I felt like God shared the smile on my face as I handed them each a giant stick of gum.

Most days, I was the top seller on the team, which helped with the underlying emptiness growing inside me. Captain was nice, but I couldn't connect with him or any of the team members like I had in the Nebraska family.

Captain gave us stationery and envelopes to write to our family. "Let them know you are happy and getting to travel," he offered as advice. Tears fell on the stationery as I wrote to my Mom and Dad, explaining how happy I was to be doing God's work. I wanted my family to be part of *the* family.

Sometimes from a phone booth, I would call the Nebraska family and talk with Crystal or Lokesh, if they were there, or whomever answered. We didn't talk for long, but I liked hearing their voices and knew they were proud of me.

I also called my "birth" family in York every few weeks, and usually talked to my mom. She always sounded worried and a little angry. It was always the same questions: "Where are you? When are you coming home, Honey?" I always tried to talk to her about how important the mission was and tried to help her understand that I was a missionary for God. The conversations were always strained. I called collect, so they would get the blessing of paying for the call.

There was a mailing address in New York we were told to give our birth family when they ask for an address. When letters were sent to that address they were opened and read, and then sent to our team captains. It was for our protection from Satan, we were told.

After about four months of fundraising, we received word that we were all being called back to Barrytown to go through a special training. We left for New York immediately.

CHAPTER 9

IN MY LIFE
The Beatles

ARRIVING AT BARRYTOWN for the second time, after being on the MFT, I felt less like a child in awe and more like an ant in a colony. I knew my way around the buildings and was familiar with the energy and atmosphere.

I was assigned a cot and had only a few minutes before dinner. My team sat together at one of the long tables in the cafeteria. I saw Toshiko across the room. I waved excitedly, and she nodded her head and smiled in acknowledgment, continuing to talk to the sister next to her. An announcement was made during dinner that Colonel Pak, Father's translator and a key figure in the organization, would be speaking to us the following day, and that we should spend the evening in prayer to prepare ourselves.

When we finished eating, Captain instructed us to meet him outside on the lawn in 30 minutes for prayer service. Throughout the chilly evening, I wished I had worn a sweater as we stood under the stars that night praying. I was tired, cold and homesick. I felt guilty for my complaining heart, but as the time passed could only think about how much I wanted to go inside. When I was finally in my sleeping bag, on my cot, I repented and cried myself to sleep. I wanted to go home to the Nebraska center but knew I was God's soldier and had to succeed at my mission.

The prayer session was the last time we were together as a team.

The next morning everyone gathered in the gym. A big white room with wood floors, a stage had been constructed against one end with a chalkboard on the wall behind it. It was the same room in which I had spent a few days before being sent off to the MFT. We sat in the normal configuration, on our knees in rows, divided by gender.

We stood when Colonel Pak entered the room. "Good morning. Please be seated," he said making bowing motions to greet us. We resumed our position back on the floor, on our knees. "I have big news for you." I knew it was good news by his big smile. "You will all be staying at Barrytown for the next four months to attend a 120-day training to become missionaries." He then explained to us how important we were to Father's mission and told us that Ken Sudo would be our teacher during our time at Barrytown. By the end of the 120 days, he said, we would be ready for our missions. What it meant to be a missionary was left vague at that point, but I had heard stories from Lokesh about how he started out as a missionary, when he was sent to Nebraska to open up a center. I imagined what it would be like to be sent out to open a center. As self-doubt arose, I told myself that God knew I was 18 years old and would help me.

Numerology is an important part of the teachings of the Divine Principle. We were taught that God worked in an orderly way and that his process of restoration was based on certain numbers. This was backed up by quotes from the Bible. The number 12 was a very important number in the "process of restoration." Colonel Pak made a point of emphasizing the importance of making every day of the 120-day period an offering to God. He was very stern, but would pepper his speech with occasional light-hearted jokes about Mr. Sudo or about being attacked by sleep spirits. His smile in those moments would transform the mood of the room from serious, almost militaristic, to warm and family-like. I was happy to be part of the "heavenly army" and determined to make God proud of me every day.

That afternoon I was assigned to a group of twenty sisters whose "Central Figure"—a term used to designate hierarchical order—was a sister by the name of Ann. A Japanese sister was Ann's own Central Figure. As in all cases since I left Nebraska, Americans were in a position to learn from the Japanese. I moved my things into a room on a different floor of the building than I had slept on the night before. Our days began with the sound of a guitar and someone singing a wake-up song like "Red, Red Robin."

I hated it. There was something about the sister who sang in the mornings that was really irritating to me. I had to begin each day repenting for my desire to tell her to shut up. "Everyone hurry outside to exercise," she said in a perky voice after the song. A Korean brother led the exercise session, which started at 6AM. We went to breakfast after that, then to the training room.

I thought Mr. Sudo was adorable. He was short, less than five feet tall. A special platform had to be made so that he could write on the chalkboard. He had a round, expressive face. His English was good, but he had an accent and sometimes had to stop and think about what the right translation of a word was. I thought of him as being "all heart." When he talked about the True Parents, he reminded me of a little boy who was absolutely in awe of his elders.

The lectures began with the topic of God. For hours, Mr. Sudo talked with dramatic animation about how wonderful God is and how much we all want to have a personal relationship with him. He described how it was possible to understand the beauty of God through a flower or through snow on a mountain. Then, after drawing us into the beauty of the world, his arms raised to the splendid sky he had painted for us, he stopped suddenly and dramatically. "But we want more than that," he yelled. "We really want to hug God." He wrapped his arms around himself and hugged and squeezed himself, as if embracing his long lost lover, and then dramatically said, "But we cannot." Then with sadness in his eyes, he slowly unfolded his arms and in a soft, almost tearful tone, added, "We cannot hug God...we lost God."

This all led to the key point, which was that we needed to pay indemnity to meet God, because when the fall of man happened, we became the children of Satan. The only reason we were gathered in the room was because of the indemnity our ancestors paid so that we could become the disciples of the Messiah. The only way back to God was through the True Parents and through our blood, sweat and tears for God.

Day after day, he passionately conveyed the story of human history, always infused with examples of how Satan is at work in our lives, all the time, trying to stop the Messiah from building the Kingdom of Heaven on earth. Between lectures there was often unison prayer. The room would fill with the sound of all of us talking to God at the same time and build with fervor and emotion.

Sometimes at the end of a prayer session I felt light-headed. It reminded me of when I used to do drugs. I was high on God.

One day, a sister I had never met ran up to me with a message that my brother had called, that it was an emergency, and I needed to call him back. My team mother, Ann, came with me to the phone to make the call.

"What's your relationship like with your family?" Ann asked as we were walking.

"I've tried so hard to get them to understand." I started to feel my throat tighten and tears begin to form. "But they just try to talk me into coming home every time I talk to them. It's like the truth is right in front of them and they can't see it."

Ann linked her arm to mine and pulled me closer to her. "You have to stay strong." She stopped and looked me in the eyes. "You are very important to God and Satan will try to invade. Are you going to be all right?"

I assured her I would be strong, and we walked to the phone arm in arm. She waited by my side while I talked to my oldest brother, Larry.

"Diane?" he asked when he heard my voice. "Honey, I have some bad news." There was silence. "Mom has breast cancer." I didn't know what to say. Silently I began to pray. "She's having surgery next week. You need to come home right away."

"I can't," I replied without hesitation. I paused, then continued, "The best thing I can do for her is to stay here and work for God."

Ann was listening to me a few steps away. I glanced at her for support but kept praying.

"What do you mean you can't come home? I just told you that Mom has cancer!"

"I'll be praying for her," I explained.

"You know what?" With disgust in his voice, he said, "If you can't come home for this, don't bother coming back ever. You aren't part of this family."

I felt like I had been punched in the chest, and tears suddenly began streaming down my cheeks. Finally the words "God needs me" pushed their way through my vocal cords in a quiet, almost whispered voice. The phone clicked.

I drew the receiver away from my ear and stared at it. Ann came over and took the phone from my hand. Through my sobs, I told her what Larry had said.

"You did the right thing. God will take care of her now." Ann tried to console me, but still it was some time before I could speak or move. I thought of Mr. Sudo hugging himself, wanting to hug God. I wanted to hug God.

"They really aren't my family," I finally said. It didn't hurt so much anymore as I said those words. "This is my family."

That man on the phone wasn't my brother, I repeated several times in my head, but Ann was my sister. I was a disciple of Christ. That was my identity. My birthday really was the day I joined the "family."

I received a letter several weeks later from my Mom letting me know she had made it through the surgery all right and that the doctors thought they got all the cancer. I also received a letter from my spiritual mother, Crystal, around the same time. She wanted me to know that one of the members from the Nebraska family, Dwight, had been fundraising with a bucket of flowers and that someone in a car called him over and said he would buy them all. He asked Dwight if he knew someone named Diane as he took all of the flowers from the bucket. Dwight said yes and the man broke all the stems off and threw the flowers down and said, "That was for what you did to Diane." I was sure it was Larry. I knew he was possessed by Satan and fasted for three days to pay indemnity for the sin he had committed in my name.

My focus on the lectures and the sincerity of my prayers grew stronger with this news. And Mr. Sudo continued to speak to us every day. With each day, history took on new meaning, as did all aspects of life. We were in an historic battle between good and evil, between God and Satan.

Sleep spirits were ever present in the lecture room. During lectures, evil spirits would pull our eyelids down so that we wouldn't hear God's words. There were lots of them hanging around the lecture hall. We fought them, though. Brothers would slug other brothers if they saw them nodding off—hard. You could hear a thud from across the room. Stabbing your leg with a pen was a technique often used. Sisters tended to take a gentler approach of nudging or massaging the neck of the person next to them to keep them awake.

One day, I smelled urine during a lecture and realized that a sister next to me obviously couldn't hold her need to go to the bathroom. I saw her try to sop up the pee with her skirt, looking around, hoping no one would notice. I felt sorry for her, but in another way proud that she had been so dedicated to God that she was willing to fight Satan that hard to stay in the room and hear God's word. I pretended I didn't notice, and never said anything to her about it.

During the weeks of lectures, we had many prayer sessions outside at night. Sometimes there were special "conditions." God was able to work best when his laws of numerology were recognized. Three, seven, twelve and forty were all important numbers, so we would often pray for 40 minutes or sometimes three hours. It didn't matter if it was cold or raining. It was actually better when it was. Then, we could pay indemnity and feel God's suffering heart better.

Numerology became so ingrained in me that when I took a drink of water I would count the number of swallows and make sure to swallow a good number, usually seven. I counted steps. I even counted the seconds it took to wash my hands.

When we had been through 40 days of lectures, it was time to go to the city to practice street preaching. My team climbed into vans, along with everyone else in the training, and descended on Manhattan. As we entered the city, the words to the song "America" played in my head:

Standing on the corner of a city I had dreamed of visiting so many times while listening to Simon and Garfunkel, I fought with Satan for making me feel sorry for myself, because I knew I would not get to explore it. I stood there instead with two other members—our assignment, to preach to passersby about how sinful the world was and how we needed God to come back into our lives.

The brother who was there with me, Stewart, whom I had never spoken with before, took charge immediately. Older than me by at least five years, he was probably about 23 years old. His wavy blond hair was a little longer than most of the brothers. He was wearing the standard shirt and tie, but crumpled. His glasses were broken and held together with a paper clip. As the van drove away, he decided we should all pray together. We stood in a circle and prayed out loud. He screamed his prayer, veins protruding from his neck and food stuck in his teeth. Self-conscious, I was very aware that people were staring at us like we were crazy.

Stewart suggested that we split up and each take a corner of the intersection. I looked at the other sister, Kim, for reassurance. My best friend from grade school's name was Kim. I missed her, wishing we were there together making fun of the food in Stewart's teeth. This Kim was tall and lanky. She stood there a bit hunched over with a panicky look on her face, telling me she was as nervous as I felt and providing no relief.

I shook off the memory of grade school Kim when she quickly agreed with Stewart and walked across the street. Stewart started screaming like a southern preacher. Kim, however, started out quietly. I watched both of them for a few awkward minutes, feeling guilty that I wasn't preaching. Finally I started saying whatever came to mind.

"God is working to build the Kingdom of Heaven," I began. "We all need to listen to God's plan." A woman pulled her child in closer and away from me like I was dangerous. "This is the most important time in history," I continued, trying to make eye contact with people, but consistently they averted their eyes the moment they met mine.

After 15 minutes or so of what felt like torture, I started to cry. It wasn't because I was moved deeply by God's plight, as I knew I should be feeling. It was because I was failing miserably. All I could think of was how foolish I looked. Eventually, I began to feel grateful that everyone walking by tried their best to ignore me, and I stopped trying to make eye contact.

Stewart and Kim didn't bother looking my direction to see how I was doing, and I was thankful. Their arms were both flailing away and the words God and Satan came from their corners every few seconds. "God has a plan," I began, and started telling the story of the fall of man and how God had been working. No one was listening, and it was more like storytelling than preaching, but it got me through.

The van finally came and we drove out of the city, back to Barrytown and more lectures. I wondered how my friend Kim was and if I would ever see her again.

Moon came to visit us several times while we were going through the training session. This training was to prepare us to be leaders, to open new centers across America, to become missionaries like Lokesh. Over and over I told myself that God knew I was 18 and would help me.

When Father talked to us, he made sure we understood how important our mission was. I watched his face as he spoke, memorizing his every expression. I had seen him speak in public before. It was different than when he spoke to us. He would swing his arms and move around the stage. Sometimes he would push or kick Mr. Sudo or anyone else who was on the stage to make a point. I felt privileged that he trusted us enough to allow us to see him as a person, not just a public figure. I loved when his eyes softened and suddenly his otherwise round and flat face changed, his cheekbones rising to allow a full, teeth-exposing smile. It was warm and fatherly. During those moments, there was kindness in his eyes, but at other times, he demonstrated such fervor, and such determination to do God's will. When his anger rose, his eyes became piercing and the muscles around his mouth clenched tight. I made a point of memorizing his facial expressions, knowing I would miss him when I was on my next mission.

As we moved into the third month of the training, the lectures focused more closely on the details of the doctrine of the Divine Principle and less on guidance for our lives. The lectures went through the teachings in a similar order as I had originally heard them from Lokesh, except in much greater detail. It was difficult to sit on the floor every day, and, for me, the sleep spirits were especially strong during these less animated lectures.

We learned in detail how God had been working through each of his Central Figures throughout history. Jesus was the most important figure in history and the most tragic. It was clear how Jesus's mission had failed. It was simple: his followers betrayed him. Jesus wasn't to blame. He did what he was supposed to do. It was all because of the people in the exact position we were in now that so much suffering had followed. All the suffering humanity had endured could have been prevented. We could have been one with God again instead of having to endure 2,000 more years of war and anguish under the invisible reign of Satan. We would all be one big family under God if only Jesus followers would have been more loyal. I knew I would never betray my True father.

We cried together as we prayed each day at the end of the lectures, linking arms and swaying back and forth, singing a Holy Song.

Urie so Wonun Tongil.
Ggumedo so wonun tongil.

We sang first in Korean, then English.

Our cherished hopes are for unity.
Even our dreams are for unity,
We'd give our lives for unity,
Come along unity.

It wasn't until toward the end of the training that Mr. Sudo announced that a new MFT was being formed: Father's Task Force. I was to be part of that group. This task force would be the front line of God's heavenly army.

It was hard to believe I would be going back to the MFT. At the same time, I was relieved to not have to go open a new center, fearing I would fail from lack of life experience. Besides, we weren't just any fundraisers; we were the special task force for Father.

CHAPTER 10

OKLAHOMA
Oscar Hammerstein

ONE HUNDRED AND TWENTY DAYS had passed, and it was time to leave Barrytown and get to work. Within the newly created fundraising teams, regions were formed and team captains were announced for each region. Standing in the lecture hall, team captains called out the names of the members of their teams. I heard my name called and walked across the room, joining the southern region.

My captain's name was Martin. He had a big smile and a round face. Like all the brothers, he wore a shirt and tie. His shirt was white and crisply pressed. He was of medium height and build with dark thick hair. He stood there like a proud peacock, perfect posture and chest expanded. As I approached, he reached for my hand and shook it like I had won a contest. Immediately, I liked him.

Team mothers were also assigned. Mine was a sister by the name of Margaret.

Our first destination would be northern Oklahoma. There were three large vans for us with a total of 16 members. The regional director was a Japanese member, and there was also a Japanese sister who was his assistant. They weren't coming with us, but would be visiting the teams in the region regularly. The vans were packed full and ready to go within a few hours after teams were assigned. One of the vans contained cases of candy that filled it almost completely.

Martin set an excited, confident tone for our team. During the long drive to Oklahoma from upstate New York, once again we each talked about our stories of joining, in ritual-like fashion. Somehow Martin was able to tease out bits of personality in each of us. We sang a lot and took turns reading from *Master Speaks.*

Martin had been a drama major in college and sometimes had us sing show tunes. It seemed unusual and almost wrong to me. But he was the captain; God was working through him. So, I allowed myself to enjoy what I would have otherwise viewed as ungodly. When we crossed the Oklahoma state border, we learned the song "Oklahoma" in three-part harmony. We were encouraged to sleep as much as possible as we made our way to our territory, so that we could get right to work when we arrived.

For the first few weeks, we worked our way through small towns, like a platoon at war, selling boxes of Thin Mints and carnations. Martin would go pick up more product while we were out selling. I had no idea what the logistics were regarding product distribution, but it was somehow arranged through the regional commander, Martin's "Central Figure." He drove around the area, familiarizing himself with each town we came to, deciding where he would drop each of us off and how long it should take us to work any particular area. He had a notebook in which he would write things down. Martin was always encouraging, even when we didn't do very well. Margaret would go out selling with each of us to see if she could offer suggestions. I was happy to be on the team and became a teacher's pet to both Martin and Margaret. I did everything I could to be helpful and, as before, was consistently a high seller.

The back of the van was always filled with product, either candy or plastic trashcans of flowers that Captain had prepared for us. Each bucket contained bunches of different colored carnations. Carnations were the most durable flowers, which is why we used them. Still, there was pressure to sell them all before they started to look bad. They were a dollar apiece or ten dollars per dozen. We always asked for donations, even if the person we were trying to sell to did not want any of what we had for sale. By the end of the day, my bag was usually heavy with change.

As we drove to a new territory at the end of the day, we prepared the money to be sent to Father. Bills were once again bundled in various amounts and wrapped with a paper strap. Coins were slid into paper coin wrappers. I have large hands and could take a handful of quarters and shake them with one hand cupped over the other, until they laid flat in the palm of one hand, and could almost always estimate correctly when I had the exact number to fit in a wrapper. I would count them and slide them in the wrapper, closing both ends. It reminded me of how I had perfected rolling joints, and I felt like I was restoring the sins of my past when I did it.

When we traveled long distances to a different part of our territory, we would do so during the night. Sometimes we would use the cases of candy as a platform for the back part of the van, and the sisters would lie on top as we drove, fitting between the roof of the van and the product. We called that a sister sandwich. The brothers would sit in the front and sleep sitting up.

I was on that team for almost a year. We would meet up with different teams on holidays and sometimes members were traded. Margaret left to go to another team after a few months and a Japanese sister joined us. She was very strict and Martin seemed different when she was there—not as playful, more nervous.

Whenever I was starting to get homesick, I called the Nebraska center. It was helpful just to hear one of the Nebraska member's voices, especially Crystal or Lokesh's. I would also call my birth Mom and Dad. Mostly I wrote them letters, though. I hated to hear how worried Mom sounded, and I resented the fact that they weren't interested in the Divine Principle.

We fundraised every day except on the four Holy days: Parent's Day, Children's Day, Day of All Things and God's Day. It was hard to find places to go on days like Thanksgiving and Christmas, which we didn't celebrate. We usually went door to door on those days in neighborhoods. One Thanksgiving, a woman made a plate of food for me and gave it to me on a paper plate. It was important to accept offerings like that since God would bless her for giving to one of his disciples. I ate every last bite and joked with the team when I got back in the van, recounting the story and making sure they knew that it was for her sake that I ate it. They teased me about how "sacrificial" I was to eat a fabulous plate of food. What I didn't say was that I was very homesick for my family as I ate it, especially my mom, and actually started to cry because I missed her and the rest of my "birth" family so much.

On Holy days we would gather by region. There was always a ceremony and a feast. Sometimes, during nice weather, we would play games like volleyball or Frisbee. We always had Korean food and an abundance of fruit, as well as sweet things like cake and cookies.

Father came to our region during one of the holidays. We clustered around him and he talked with us in a very intimate way. He didn't stay long, but it made us realize how much he cared about us.

During that gathering, there was a meeting of team captains. The regional commander then called us together and read names off a piece of paper, assigning everyone to new teams. I would be going to Louisiana. A former teammate would be my new captain.

Chapter 11

Back on the Chain Gang
The Pretenders

THERE WAS A KNOCK on the door of the Texaco station women's bathroom that awakened me with a start. "I'll be right out," I said automatically. Looking at my watch I realized I had been sleeping for over an hour, sitting on the toilet. My case of Thin Mints was on my lap; my head had been resting on my folded arms. "I'm sorry, Father," I whispered desperately as I stood up to leave.

I was wearing a pair of polyester pants that were a little too short, a cotton flowered shirt and running shoes. My hair looked as though I had cut it myself. It was short and held back to one side with a hairpin. I was wearing no make-up. Looking in the mirror for a moment as I prepared to leave, I felt like crying. The extra weight, the K-Mart clothes, the hair... Pushing back the tears, I remembered the morning chant: "We are God's soldiers and this is the front line."

I placed the strap of my bag over my head so that it hung across my chest to the opposite hip. Picking up my case of candy and positioning it under the other arm, I was ready for battle. I opened the door with my free hand and began to run to the hardware store next door chanting under my breath as I ran. "We are God's soldiers and this is the front line... We are God's soldiers and this is the front line... We are God's soldiers and this is the front line... We are God's soldiers..." I knew I would have to work fast to make up for lost time.

When my new Captain—Jonas—picked me up, he seemed frantic. He told me Carol was an hour late for her pick-up. We drove back to the area she had been working. He pulled into a strip mall and ran inside a flower store. I saw him talking to a woman behind the counter. She pulled out a box of mints from behind the counter and showed them to him. When he got back into the van, he told me she had been there several hours ago. We drove further down the road and pulled into another parking lot. "Go ask the guy in there if he saw her," he said, pointing to a car wash. "I'll go ask in there." We both got out of the van.

"I saw a girl get pushed into a blue van right over there," the attendant told me. "I would have called the police, but I heard her call one of the women Mom, so I figured she was a runaway."

"Did you get a license plate?" I asked.

"I was busy with a customer. I told you the van was blue, that's all I remember."

I ran to find Jonas and shared what I found out. He went to a phone booth to call Commander at the regional headquarters in Houston.

When he came back to the van, I could tell by the look on his face that I wasn't going to hear any good news. "Carol hasn't called in. I was told to call back in an hour," Greg told me. "Commander Hyashi wasn't there." He took off his glasses and put them on the dash. He clenched his hands together hard and raised them to his bent head to pray. The muscles in his head pulled tight. He looked scared. I couldn't help but feel like it was somehow his fault.

I resented that he was my Captain. We had worked together several months prior on the same team in Texas. I always generated more money for Father's work than he did and I hated that he was so into sports. There was a newspaper opened to the sports page stuck between the driver's seat and the console between the seats. I could see no place for football in building the Kingdom of Heaven.

Jonas looked at his watch when he had finished praying and began picking up the rest of the team. At one point, he stopped at another phone booth. He was on the phone quite a while. Neither of us said anything about Carol until everyone was in the van. We pulled over after the last team member got in, and he told everyone that it was likely deprogrammers had kidnapped Carol. We all knew deprogrammers were Satan's front line soldiers trying to destroy us. They snatched members and tore down their faith, drawing them back into his evil, Godless world of sin.

That night, we didn't go back out. After the money was counted and put away, we went to a city park and had a four-hour prayer condition for Carol. We joined hands and sang several Holy Songs, Jonas prayed, we prayed in unison, and then we went off by ourselves to pray alone. When we came back together, Jonas told us that Commander Hyashi said we should work especially hard to pay indemnity. Paying indemnity was a way to give power to good spirits who were fighting evil spirits. We could offer our indemnity to those spirits who were working to save Carol from Satan's powers.

I felt anxious the next morning as the team members were being given their areas to work. The night before I had promised, in prayer, that I would set a goal of 200 dollars for the day. It had been a while since I had set a goal that high, but I felt somehow responsible for what had happened to Carol.

I knew I had a Cain/Abel problem with Jonas. So much time had been spent during our lectures in Barrytown on how we would be challenged by the same dynamics that caused Cain to kill his brother Abel, and now here I was facing that precise predicament. I knew I should blindly respect Jonas, since he was chosen to be my leader. But still, I couldn't bring myself to call him Captain. I did everything I could to not call him anything.

I was the last one remaining in the van when Jonas pulled into a parking lot. He told me he wanted to talk. He shut off the van and turned around to face me. I was sitting on the bench seat behind him. "Why don't you come up here?" he said, slapping the passenger seat next to him. I climbed into the front.

"I haven't told the rest of the team yet," he started, "but Father has set a 21-day competition, starting the day after tomorrow."

My body sank at the idea. I knew what that meant. Twenty-one days of push. Now I knew why he wanted to talk to me alone; I had been one of the top sellers on the entire MFT at times. I was waiting for a, "God is counting on you to set an example" speech.

Jonas pushed his glasses up the bridge of his nose. "What is it that's bothering you, Diane? When we were in Texas, you seemed like a different person."

I wanted to say something like *I had a real Captain then* or *just let me out and go read your sports section*. But I didn't. Instead I reminded myself that God works through hierarchy. I had to support Jonas to get to God, or I would repeat the sin of Cain. So I didn't answer, and he finally broke the silence.

"I think this team has a chance of winning. What can I do to help you do well?" I watched him push his glasses up again. "I want to help you if I can." He seemed sincere.

Suddenly, something washed over me. He didn't seem so bad after all. I looked at his crumpled shirt and knew he was working really hard and that he felt horrible about Carol. At that moment, he seemed like a fidgety little boy playing grown-up. I looked at the picture of Father taped to the front of the dash, took a deep breath and said, "I guess I've been feeling sorry for myself. When we were at the last regional meeting, I was praying for a different mission. I've been on the MFT for over a year now and I had been praying to God to send me back to my home state to work there again." Tears started to form in my eyes.

Jonas began to look around in the van for tissues. Spotting some in the back seat, he quickly climbed between the seats to get them, knocking over an open case of candy in the process and bumping his head trying to stop it from falling. My tears turned to laughter for a moment. Jonas smiled and threw me the tissue box, picked up the candy and put it back in the case, then climbed back into the driver's seat, rubbing his head where he bumped it.

"I'll be all right," I assured him. "Thanks for asking."

He drove me to my area and I got out with my candy. I felt a wave of strength and summoned enough courage to face the challenge ahead. I took the photo of Father and Mother out of my bag, the one Crystal had given me when I left Nebraska, and held it to my chest. The edges were a bit ragged. I put it back and began to sing a Holy Song as I hurried toward the factory ahead. I had done well in industrial areas in the past. "Marching on heavenly soldiers. Marching on with his love. United in life eternal with the God of Heaven and earth," I sang. My free hand made a fist and pounded the air to the beat of the song.

We had driven a few miles from the place we had stopped to talk and there was nothing around for miles except a huge sugar factory. I had learned over time how to get into just about any place and sell as much as I could before getting told it was against the rules.

When we debriefed our days, we always shared with each other the ways we'd developed for tricking Satan. For instance, when we needed to get into a secured building we would ring several doorbells. When someone asked who it was, we would say we had a delivery, and then go to another floor when we got in the building, or just go in when someone else was walking in. In restaurants, we would walk in and spot someone in the back of the restaurant and then say to the hostess, "Oh, there's my friend." Then, we would walk back to that table and try to sell to them, and proceed to as many tables as possible until we got kicked out. Sometimes at a buffet I would go in and eat, then start selling until I got kicked out, never paying for my food.

Now, at the factory, I had a case of candy resting on one hip, as usual, and my bag strapped over my head and falling to the other hip. I saw the door to the main office and decided to go there last.

I walked around the outside of the buildings. There were big holding tanks and pipes billowing white steam into the air. I saw a door with a sign showing the number of days since an accident and hard hats hanging on hooks in a row outside the door. "Hardhat Area" was written in big red letters above the door; I took a hardhat and went inside. I approached the first person I saw and told him it was his lucky day.

"Why is that?" he asked.

"You get to buy some candy and help the church."

"Oh, I do?" he said, cocking his head, like he was going to argue with me about that, but then he just smiled and reached for his wallet. "How much?"

Since being in Louisiana, I had discovered that if I said "the church" no one questioned which one. I even learned a little Spanish. *Dulces para la iglesia. Uno por dos; tres por cinco.* Candy for the church. One for two; three for five. I knew most Spanish-speaking people in that area assumed I meant the Catholic Church. They would be so happy one day when they realized it was for the second coming of Christ, and that they had made the most important offering to God of their life. I imagined their ancestors watching and celebrating from Spirit World.

I made my way through room after room of giant vats and gears and rollers and big metal tubes selling candy to almost everyone I came across. Eventually, a supervisor told me I wasn't supposed to be in that area and that I should go to the main office and ask if I could wait in the lunch room. The whistle was about to blow for lunch, he told me. He pointed me toward the office and I headed that way. Along the way I saw what looked like it could be the lunchroom he had been talking about. I went there instead. I sold out my case of candy during lunch and headed back to meet up with Captain.

I broke $300 that day. Captain told us about the competition that night and we had a special prayer service to offer ourselves fully to the competition.

We worked hard, but ran into legal problems in some of the small towns in southern Louisiana. There were non-solicitation laws that required a permit for anyone to sell in the town. Several of us were arrested. A Police car slowed down as I was walking down the sidewalk carrying my box of candy. They rolled down the window to talk to me and I saw one of my teammates in the back seat. He stopped and opened the door for me to get in. The officers took us to the station. I made the call to headquarters. We waited for over an hour for Captain to come and bail us out.

My battle with not wanting to be on the MFT continued. Satan seemed to always invade my mind with thoughts of what else I could do with my life, instead of humbly following God's given path for me. I was so tired of selling. I knew it was wrong to ask anything of God. I should be asking how I could serve him better, but I found myself pleading with him in my prayers to let me work for him somewhere else than the MFT. I knew the number 40 was symbolic of separation from Satan, so I decided to do a 40-hour selling condition to prove to God that I was ready for a new mission.

I didn't tell Captain why I was doing it. He thought it was just about the competition. He reluctantly agreed to let me work through the night, to not rest for 40 hours.

It was difficult to find a place to put me in the middle of the night. After driving around for awhile Captain finally drove me to a truck stop for the night. "See you in the morning" he said before driving away. Sometime around four in the morning, I fell asleep leaning against a wall. I woke up as I started to fall over. The next day, I started to fall asleep while walking across a parking lot at a grocery store. By then, I had been awake for about 30 hours. I caught myself nodding off all day. It wasn't my best day making money, but I still made more than anyone else on the team.

Our team didn't win the competition, but I was one of the top sellers in the country. A few days after the competition Captain picked up a package at the post office from headquarters. "This is for you," he told me when I got in the van, pointing to a package. That night at prayer service he gave me the package. It was a prize for being a top seller. I opened it and saw a signed 8x10 picture of Father. Really it was two pictures, which were taken at his speaking tour at Washington Monument. One was of the crowds; the other was a close-up of Father speaking. He was wearing a suit and a tie and looked very serious as he delivered his speech. That picture was signed. Both pictures were in a leather-like frame that folded together in two.

After doing so well in the competition, I was also chosen to be on an elite team for the next three months. I don't remember where we were. It was all a blur and it didn't matter where we were anyway. All that mattered was where that next person was who would buy a box of candy.

Margaret was on the team. I was really happy to see her and to get the chance to work so closely with her. She felt like a real friend, like an older sister who truly cared about me. I had a bit of a crush on her. As a team, we all made record-breaking amounts. I made over $600 one day, the most I ever made.

I confided in Margaret, telling her that I wanted to do something else besides fundraise. I had thought it through and was sure that if I could go back to school I would be more useful to God. She was compassionate, but was quick to remind me that I needed to trust in God's plan for me.

CHAPTER 12

MOTHER AND CHILD REUNION
Paul Simon

A FEW DAYS AFTER THE CONVERSATION about my hope to go to school, we were told we were needed in New York to help our brothers and sisters prepare for Yankee Stadium. Father would be speaking there in a matter of weeks, so it was crucial that the stadium be full. This was part of God's plan to restore failures of the past and to prepare the world to welcome the messiah.

The church had just acquired a major piece of real estate in Manhattan, the New Yorker Hotel. We would be staying there. Walking through the front door, and feeling the buzz of the hive, suddenly rekindled my confidence that soon the world would know the good news: Christ was here.

I called my birth Mom and Dad and told them I would be in New York City to work on a special project for awhile. We had been instructed to try to persuade our families to come to the event. The historical significance of the event was beyond comprehension. World victory depended on 210,000 people attending. Being in the New Yorker and feeling the importance of what we were doing temporarily dissolved my obsession with getting a new mission. I felt revitalized and ignored my exhaustion.

Mr. Kamiyama was the leader in charge of the MFT and we were under his direction, once we arrived. After being around Mr. Sudo in Barrytown, I immediately realized the difference in their leadership styles. Mr. Kamiyama was more dynamic, and more militaristic. The atmosphere around him was intense and focused. After being on small fundraising teams, I felt lost among the large number of members gathered to work on Yankee Stadium. We were sent to the streets to invite people to attend the speech.

After being there a few days, I was given a message that my Mom had been trying to reach me and that I should call her. I wondered if something bad had happened. What she told me instead took me completely by surprise. She was coming to New York to see me. She explained that she would be coming with some other mothers of members from the area. There were five of them from various places in the Midwest. I had never known her to do something like this without my Dad. I wasn't sure if it was God or Satan at work. I decided it was God, but just in case, I knew I needed to be vigilant for signs of Satan at work.

The brother who was in charge of our group wasn't very interested in the fact that my Mom was coming. I didn't know what to tell her or what I was supposed to do when she got there, but didn't have much time to worry about it; I found myself completely caught up in the excitement of what we were doing. I had been assigned to a team of members that went out into different places like Brooklyn or Queens or the Bronx. We would leave early and come home late. Our mission was to convince people to come to Yankee Stadium. We were handing out invitations with coupons for a bus ride and lunch. While I couldn't come out and say the words, I wanted my spirit to tell the people I invited that The Lord or the Second Advent would be speaking, that it was better than if Jesus himself was here. But until the proper foundation was laid, we could not announce that Moon was the Messiah. Otherwise, Satan would make it seem like we were crazy and blasphemous. And it was vital that this time the Messiah be successful.

There was pressure to make our goals every day. The fate of the world was riding on this one moment. Everyone felt the urgency.

The day my Mom arrived, I was only able to see her for a little while. She wanted me to go with her, to spend the day with her.

I knew that wasn't possible. I wasn't allowed to be alone with her for fear of deprogramming. There had been a string of deprogrammings over the previous years, and I didn't trust her to not try it with me. The memory of Carol being pushed into a van and never heard from again while I was on Jonas' team was etched in my mind. Besides, I couldn't neglect my responsibilities for that long at this critical moment in human history.

She was clearly upset about this. I wanted more than anything for my family to be part of the True Family—for my whole family to be there and to see what I was a part of, how powerful we were, how obvious it was that we were working directly with God to change the world. I told my Mom I would go with her to the rally. My prayer was that she would see Father for who he was this time, unlike in Hawaii.

My plan was to meet her and go to the speech with her, but things weren't going well the day of the event and I wasn't able to meet up with her. Buses were late and there weren't enough of the boxed lunches for everyone. Then it started to rain, destroying many of the decorations at the stadium. There was no time to go back and get her. My team was busy with taking care of one problem after another all the way through the speech. When it was over, we were all afraid that we had failed. It was obvious the stadium wasn't full.

I was exhausted by the time I returned to the hotel with my team. Thinking that I would find my Mom and see what she had thought of the speech, I began to straighten my clothes and hair, but before we had a chance to get in the door we were given the news that the City of New York had given us until morning to remove all the posters we had "littered" throughout the city, or the church would be fined a very large amount.

The Central Figure I was assigned to during the event was a Japanese brother. I tried to explain to him that my Mom was inside, but his eyes were moving so fast and frantically that they never settled on mine long enough to see me as a person, let alone show any compassion for the fact that she was waiting for me. It was all about the mission. Every brother and sister available was to spend the night scraping posters from subway walls and buildings throughout the city. As I waited for his answer, his Central Figure approached and took him aside to talk with him. When he returned, he told us all to load into a van outside. There was no further discussion.

The next morning I saw Mom for a few minutes. I hadn't slept a wink and knew I looked terrible. That's all the time I had before getting in a van to go hear Father speak to us at Belvedere. She was livid. She told me she had complained to someone. She was in tears. One of the women she had come with tried to calm her. I had to go. Even though I didn't like seeing her like that, I was more frustrated than empathetic. She just didn't understand the importance of this work. It felt familiar that she didn't understand me. Still, seeing her cry was painful and I wanted to comfort her more than I could.

CHAPTER 13

EVERYBODY MUST GET STONED
Bob Dylan

YANKEE STADIUM WAS OVER and it was time to go back to our missions. I was assigned to an all-new team in the same region from where I began. It had been two years since joining the Family. Nebraska seemed a distant memory, which I thought of with the longing of a soldier in a foreign land.

Our new territory was southern Texas. This time, my captain's name was Danny. He had dark coarse hair and wore glasses. He was Italian and talked with a loud "New Yorker" voice. I immediately disliked him. I knew he was under a lot of pressure, but I had no empathy for him. Our regional commander was a Japanese brother who made it clear there was no excuse for failure.

We worked in Houston first. It was June, and the humidity stuck to my skin. I needed a shower after walking two blocks. The city seemed filthy to me and I found it hard to breathe. Nights were best, when it cooled down a bit. We did better then, going bar to bar, blitzing.

Blitzing was very fast paced. Captain would rapidly drive from bar to bar, let one or two people off, then return in 15 minutes or at most half an hour to take us to the next one. This was my favorite part of the day: God's version of bar hopping.

We had a new product, which we called bugs on sticks. These things were designed to go in flower arrangements or to be stuck in potted plants. There were different colored butterflies, dragonflies and bumblebees made of wire and silk and attached to a thin, wiry, plastic-covered stick. When you held them, they swayed. The nice thing is that they were light to carry and definitely got people's attention when you walked into a business with a handful of them. We alternated between the bugs on sticks and boxes of candy.

After a few months in Houston, we left for smaller cities like Galveston. Galveston was beautiful. Growing up in Nebraska, I had never spent any time near the ocean. My family had gone to California on vacation when I was young, but I hardly remembered seeing the ocean. It had never before occurred to me to want to stay and explore anywhere we had been fundraising, but Satan really invaded me in Galveston. I saw people enjoying themselves and wanted to be one of them.

I didn't tell anyone how I was feeling; I just prayed about it. I already had a terrible Cain/Abel problem and knew I was in the position of Cain. I reminded myself of how Cain killed his younger brother, Abel, who was closer to God, and how God had accepted Abel's offering and rejected Cain's. To restore this tragic occurrence in the history of God's dispensation, it was critical to always go through the person God had chosen. This time it was Danny, and he was the only route to God, according to the Divine Principle. I had to pray constantly for forgiveness for my negative feelings toward him and for my new desire to run away and live in Satan's world.

It was hard to approach people with enthusiasm when I just wanted to sit on the beach with friends and laugh. It was especially challenging when the sun made the waves glisten, and couples walked hand in hand on the beach. I imagined them thinking only of the moment they were in, while I sold bugs on sticks and was always in battle with Satan. I had to consider all of eternity, all the time.

Moment by moment I conquered my personal battle on the coast, and was relieved when we headed for a new location: more inland, less tempting. Still, I wasn't making as much money as previously, and was tired most days. I would look for a place to sneak in a nap almost daily, crawling into secluded stairwells or behind bushes to fall asleep for a while, and then repent for it.

One day, I was dropped off at a mall. I was supposed to work the parking lot, approaching people as they were heading to their cars. My results for the day were very low and it was nearly evening. Instead of excitement and enthusiasm, I approached people near tears. It wasn't working and I decided to go into the mall to use the bathroom and to pray.

Inside the mall the Red Cross was doing a blood drive. Seeing the donation station reminded me of prayer service the night before: Captain had read a speech from *Master Speaks*. In the speech, Father talked about the need to give blood, sweat and tears for God. The sight of the Red Cross seemed like a clear sign, so I decided to donate blood as a symbol of my dedication.

As the Red Cross nurse drew my blood, I threw up and fainted. The nurse made me stay and rest for awhile, explaining to me that some people had that reaction. By the time I was back outside, it was time to meet the Captain. I decided not to tell him what I had done. It was between God and me, I decided, pulling the sleeve down over the bandage on my arm, counting the few dollars I had made.

After the next regional Holy Day gathering, Parent's Day, our teams were shuffled some, but I was still with Danny. The Commander came with our team for a few days to observe. He told Danny we needed to do repentance conditions if we didn't make our daily goals. One of the sisters on our team, Mary, was having a really hard time. She was almost always the low seller of the team. She had severe acne and always looked down. Shortly after Commander left our team, she had a day that she hardly sold anything.

Danny had set a repentance condition that we take one minute of a cold shower for every dollar under your goal. I remember hearing Mary crying that night in the shower. She was in there for more than an hour. The next evening when we were on our way to the motel room I noticed Mary wasn't in the van. "Where's Mary?" I asked Danny. "She must have been kidnapped. She wasn't at her pick up spot. I looked for her most of the day." After a few moments of silence he added, "Please pray." I imagined she had just left on her own, and I blamed him for that.

One late night, somewhere in the heart of Texas, we were all exhausted and Danny was looking for a place to drop me off during a bar blitz. We drove down a dark highway and there was a bar down a lane, almost out of sight of the highway. A neon light led our way to it. There were several pick-ups and a row of Harleys parked outside.

"Okay, I'll be back in about half an hour or so," he said when we stopped in the parking lot, as if we were pulling up to a Dunkin' Donuts in the middle of the day. I looked at him without saying a word and got out with my box of candy. He drove off. A red beat-up pick-up was pulling in as he was leaving. A man parked and got out, wearing a cowboy hat and jeans so well worn that his can of chew had created a permanent mark in the back pocket. I decided to approach him before going in the bar.

"Excuse me, would you like to buy some candy for a non-denominational church group?" I asked him. He looked at me like I was from another planet. Then he looked at the van I had just gotten out of driving down the highway toward town, then back at me.

"Did you just get dropped off here by yourself?" he asked me.

"Yes," I said trying to sound confident, but wanting to cry.

"How old are you?"

"Nineteen," I replied, immediately wishing I had lied and said I was older.

"You're not even old enough to go in there. That's a rough place. You shouldn't be here alone." I could tell he was drunk and mad.

"I'll be okay," I told him.

"You'll be okay because I'm seein' to that," he said. "I want to have a word with whoever left you here." He crossed his arms and leaned up against his pick-up and stuffed some tobacco in his mouth. I started to open my mouth to argue as to why I should go in and try to sell my candy, but stopped as he spat out some disgusting brown tobacco juice and started talking about the "mother fucking, asshole, shitbag" who left me there. "Excuse my language," he said, after telling me again, slurringly, how dangerous it was for someone like me to be left there alone. He told me about his daughter who just had a baby boy and how he had lost his own son in a car accident.

He stayed there with me until the van pulled in the parking lot. "Thank you," I said. "I'll be okay now." I started to head for the van. The cowboy followed me. I climbed in the side door of the van, and he opened the passenger side of the van and proceeded to tell Danny what an asshole he was. Danny looked like a scared little boy about to pee his pants. He was all apologies and thank yous to the cowboy. But when we drove away he became furious—at me. The veins in his neck protruded as he yelled.

I sat in the back seat and kept my mouth shut. The last thing I expected was for him to be mad at me. I thought he would feel bad for dropping me off in such a dangerous place. "Do you realize how much danger you just put me in?" he asked me. I had no idea what he would have wanted me to do differently, how I was supposed to have protected *him*. Tired and emotional, I sat in the back seat and cried silently, wiping my tears and snot on the arm of my jacket. We drove back to pick up the rest of the team in silence. That night was never spoken of again.

The next holiday, I was taken off Danny's team. My new captain was someone I had been with when I was part of the top sellers' team. Richard—Rick—reminded me a little of Woody Allen. He had a small frame and a receding hairline. He was older than most of the MFT, maybe in his early 30s. He was very respectful of me, but I could tell as the weeks passed that he was disappointed in my results. I wanted to be enthusiastic, but couldn't find the same kind of energy inside myself that I had when we were on the top seller team together.

This was an easier team for me. I didn't have to deal with a Cain/Abel issue and there was no major competition going on. Sometimes, Rick would pick us all up early and we would do something together like go to a movie.

Certain movies were recommended by Father. As the children of the Messiah, we all wanted to do everything like Father. He liked Big Macs, so we always ate them when we went to McDonalds. He also liked pizza and ice cream, which became a typical special treat at the end of a competition.

When *Star Wars* came out, we learned that Father loved it and had instructed all members to see it. Since we interpreted everything we saw or experienced through the doctrine of the Divine Principle, movies were no exception. *Star Wars* was about the battle between God and Satan and about trusting in the power of God's will. Every night when we debriefed our day, it would be in the context of how God had prevailed or how Satan was able to invade.

I started to think a lot about how I was capable of doing more than selling two-dollar items on the street day after day, and that God had other plans for me. At one point, just before being assigned to Danny's team, I made a request to become a team captain. Toshiko had a long talk with me about what the "sister's role" is. She made sure I understood that we, as women, were in a supportive role to the brothers. That was what God had created us to do. It was just as important a role as the role men played, she said, just different. She talked to me about how one day I would be blessed and would need to support my husband. I tried to take that into my heart, knowing it was God's way. But deep down, I didn't agree that women should be limited to supporting men.

A relatively small "blessing" had just taken place when she talked to me. Seventy-four couples had received the blessing. I knew my day would come and Father would choose the perfect husband for me, but I also knew that it was important for older sisters to be blessed first. Toshiko was definitely due to be blessed. I was still only 19.

I had heard stories about the blessing of 1975. One thousand eight hundred couples were matched by Father and blessed in marriage in Korea. The brothers were in lines on one side of a large auditorium, sisters on the other. He would point to a brother and ask him to stand up, and then look around at the sisters.

Eventually, he would ask a sister to stand. Sometimes he would say, no, sit back down, and then choose someone else. When he felt it was a good match, those two would be sent to a place to have a few minutes to talk with each other. They could humbly ask for another choice, but it was looked down upon. In almost all cases, the couple would accept Father's choice and be on their way to spending their lives together—after the customary separation period. Couples were sent on separate missions for at least 40 days immediately after the blessing ceremony. Some couples would rarely see their mate, if at all, for periods of months or even years from the time of their blessing.

I respected Toshiko and knew that I should trust what she was saying, but the idea of getting blessed to a stranger was not as motivating to me as the idea of doing something else besides the MFT.

I kept the pictures of the True Parents close at hand and tried to battle the feelings I had that kept telling me that I could serve God better if I were given the chance to do something else besides fundraise. There were still occasions when I would see people having fun or just relaxing with family or friends and I would feel sorry for myself. It was never as severe as in Galveston, but the feelings would come up. I tried to remember Father's suffering course and God's sadness, both of which Mr. Sudo had made so clear to us. He had warned us that there would be days we would feel sorry for ourselves.

Whenever this came up for me, I tried to remember the time I fasted and received the revelation that I was going to be Satan's spiritual mother and that I should always look for the hardest path in order to grow my heart. I began to wonder if I was really cut out for the job.

As I was going door to door in some apartments one evening, I came to a door that had loud music coming from it. Someone came to the door with a long ponytail and bloodshot eyes. I told him what I was doing. He bought a box of candy and offered me a brownie. I knew they weren't "normal" brownies. I hesitated for a few seconds, and then took one off the plate in front of me.

"Thank you. Have a nice evening." I walked away.

"You too," he said as I walked away. "Good luck." He smiled and gave me the peace sign. I ate the brownie as soon as I was around the corner.

When I got back to the van I told Captain I wasn't feeling well. He let me sit in the back of the van and rest. I didn't repent. I was sure the guy who gave me the brownie would be blessed by God and I didn't mind making the sacrifice of being stoned for a few hours for his sake.

I had been calling Lokesh and Crystal frequently during that time. I told them that I really wanted to come back and go to school. Lokesh understood and thought school would be good for both Crystal and me. When we were in Nebraska, he had insisted on both of us getting our GEDs. We studied together and both got high scores, even though neither of us had made it past the eighth grade. I started to have some hope that I could go.

As we were working our way through small towns around Dallas, we ended up staying in the Dallas Unification Church center. The members there went on with their witnessing mission while we continued ours.

When we came home one night from selling, I needed to take a shower. There was a bathtub and I hadn't soaked in a bathtub for years. I decided to take a long bath. You would have thought I had burned down the house. There were several knocks on the door while I was in there. I just replied with, "I'm still in here." When I came out, a sister from the center asked me if I knew how selfish it was of me to have stayed in the bathroom that long. I said "sorry" and turned and walked away while she was still talking. I told Rick the next day that I had decided God wanted me to go back to the Nebraska center.

I still believed God had a special mission for me, but even if I really was supposed to be Satan's spiritual mother, I still believed that I needed to find other ways to grow my heart than fundraising.

Margaret was working in my region, floating from team to team, helping support the captains. She came to Dallas specifically to talk with me within a few days of my conversation with Rick. She told me that some things were going on in the Nebraska family that were not good. She asked me lots of questions about my time there, and told me she couldn't say much more, but that she would see if I could be assigned a new mission. She was very loving and supportive.

I felt sick. I wanted to know what was going on. I called the Nebraska center the next day and talked to Crystal. She wouldn't say any more than Margaret had said. She agreed that this was not a good time to come back, though. She needed to get off the phone quickly but had made it clear that coming back to Nebraska was not what I should do. My heart sunk.

I had developed feelings for Margaret similar to those I had felt for one of my brother's friends, Cheryl, back in York. I wanted Margaret to hold me that night when I was in my sleeping bag on the floor. I remember feeling that way when I was in York and thought of Cheryl. She was like a big sister to me, but I knew those feelings were more than I would feel for a sister. I never felt like that about boys. I didn't want to be close to them like that. I felt scared and prayed for forgiveness.

Within a few days I found myself sitting on a bus to New York City. Margaret sat with me for a few minutes at the bus station and explained that I would be staying in the New Yorker Hotel and working under Mr. Kamiyama. She gave me a hug and told me she would be praying for me. I knew I would miss her.

CHAPTER 14

ALREADY GONE
Eagles

SHORTLY AFTER MY ARRIVAL in New York, I was assigned to a team who was passing out newspapers on the street. *The News World* was one of the latest business ventures of the church. It was a city-based daily newspaper whose staff was made up of members of the church. It had been launched New Years Eve, 1977. My team's mission was trying to get people to read it by standing out on the streets of the city yelling out the headlines. "Read all about it!" we would scream out. "The paper is free today."

I was handing papers out on August 16, 1977. Everyone wanted a paper that day. "Elvis is dead," I yelled out. I felt disconnected from everything and everyone, not part of the world of people who were flocking to read about Elvis, but not connected to my mission, either. I didn't know anyone on my team and the urgency I had felt as part of the MFT was diluted on this mission. I had been hanging on to my connection to Lokesh and the Nebraska family as a place to call home, and the bridge back to that life seemed to have been burned.

One morning, after a few days of handing out papers, Mr. Kamiyama reassigned teams. New assignments were handed out. I had a new mission…fundraising. My heart sank, but I knew it was only temporary, so I didn't say anything about the fact that I had left the MFT for a *new* mission. The team consisted mostly of members who had recently joined. They were going to go to

Barrytown for a training session in a couple of weeks, but in the meantime were assigned to this team to raise money by selling candy on the streets of Manhattan. I was told I could help them, having been on the MFT. I would be going to Barrytown again, too. I got the feeling that no one knew what to do with me. I worked alongside a new sister named Sharon for several days, who had recently joined in Minnesota. I was to help with her training.

Sharon began to open up to me about her reservations about the group. She didn't dress or wear her hair in the standard way for a sister: her shirts were stylish and sometimes low cut, and she wore make-up and had long hair. She was outspoken about how it shouldn't matter how you dress, as long as you work for God. She trusted me, and I took it upon myself to be a big sister to her. I told her she would like the training in Barrytown and would understand more about the organization.

One morning, when it was time for the team to gather to go out to the streets with our candy, I noticed Sharon wasn't there. When we came back to the hotel, she was standing outside the door crying.

"What's going on?" I asked her.

"They kicked me out, just told me to leave without a penny in my pocket. I'm not even allowed to go inside the building," she told me. She looked scared and was really upset. Her boyfriend had come to see her and she went with him for the day. I asked her if they had sex and she admitted she had. "I just don't understand," she said. "I still want to work for God. I told him it was over and to go home. It was just one last day together. We went to his hotel room and it just kinda happened. I don't see why it's such a big deal." I tried to comfort her and to explain why it was a big deal, but I was upset about how she was being treated.

When she returned to the hotel, a Japanese sister questioned her. Then she was escorted out of the building and told she was not allowed back inside. She didn't have a dime to her name or even a change of clothes. Her boyfriend had caught a flight back to Minnesota that afternoon. She didn't know what to do. She didn't want to be a member anymore, though, she knew that much. She said she would find another way to serve God.

I told Sharon to wait while I went inside. I was determined to find Mr. Kamiyama and talk to him about this. Even if she wasn't a member, she needed a safe way to get home. I wasn't permitted to talk directly to him. One of the top American brothers named Paul tried to calm me down. He promised to take care of things. He knew I was really upset but told me the situation had to be handled through the proper hierarchy.

"She's out on the streets of New York City without any money, crying. It will be dark soon. This isn't right," I said.

"Okay, I understand," he assured me. He promised he would take care of it and told me I needed to go back and join my team. I went back outside first to tell Sharon that someone would be out to help her. I wanted to stay with her, but knew I had to go with my team. I trusted Paul.

The next morning I found Paul. "Sharon was given bus fare and a few dollars for food and to call home" he told me. I was relieved and thanked him. Paul looked like an all-American boy, with his blond hair and baby face. A rising star in the organization, he talked to me with a kind, reassuring voice. Paul seemed to have a way of bridging the cultural difference between the Japanese style we called kamikaze and the American, more laid back style of leadership.

Joining my team, I felt disconnected from all of them. The team captain was a Japanese brother, trained under Mr. Kamiyama. This must be what book camp is like in the army, I thought. Captain barked orders at us, without eye contact. He handed each of us a box of candy and said simply, "Go. Sell." As we headed out the door he said, "Be back here at 6:00." I started down the street, not knowing how to approach people in Manhattan. It was very different from Texas. I hung out with other street vendors for awhile. Some of them had tables or display cases that could be folded up and made to look like a briefcase or small suitcase in a matter of seconds. It was illegal to sell goods on the street, so they would watch the vendor next to them and as soon as they saw them folding up they would do the same. It was like dominoes. There would be a line of vendors one minute, with watches and jewelry nicely displayed, and the next minute those same people would be walking down the street like anyone else the next, not a vendor in sight.

Standing there on the street, I watched a man with a suit and a briefcase walk by with a woman in a blue dress, where the vendors used to be. They hurried into a building, him glancing at his watch, her sipping coffee from a paper cup. I wondered how they became the people with important meetings to go to and real documents in their briefcases instead of fake watches, like the vendors.

I walked into an office building and went to the elevator. I pushed a random number and the doors opened to a floor that was being remodeled. No one was working there that day, though. I got out and walked around. There were half-finished walls and piles of drywall stacked next to them. I opened a door into a room that was carpeted and looked finished, except that it was still unfurnished. I sat down and leaned against the wall. The box of candy was sitting on my outstretched legs and I folded my arms on top of it to rest my head on, as I had many times before. I dozed off for a few minutes, then stood up and put the box down and walked over to the window. I thought about Paul and Sharon and Lokesh and my years on the MFT. It suddenly occurred to me that I needed to talk to Paul. I was done fundraising. I was done that very minute. Falling asleep on boxes of candy was not the best I could do for God. I was ready to stand up for what I knew to be true. I knew I needed to go to school, to fill my briefcase with something real. I stood there looking out the window planning my strategy. A prayer began to leave my lips and I was certain God was listening. I promised him that I would make him proud.

I picked up my case of candy and headed back to the New Yorker. It was hours before I was scheduled to meet the rest of the team there. I felt powerful in my certainty. I would prove to God that I could do great things for him.

When I found Paul I told him I needed to talk with him. That it was important. We sat in the lobby of the hotel and talked. I explained to him about my talks with Margaret and how I ended up in New York. I also told him about the Nebraska family and how I didn't know what was going on but that I knew I couldn't go there. I just need to go to school, I explained. I asked about CARP, the Collegiate Association for the Research of Principles. I didn't know much about it, except that it was for recruiting students and that the centers were run by members who were going to school.

"That would be great, but those are students who join while they are in school. That's very different than your situation," Paul explained. "The church doesn't pay for their school or living expenses. You know how important Father's work is; we can't take Father's money for your school."

I understood about the money and had thought about it. I was very grateful that Paul wasn't lecturing me about being more humble and blindly following God's plan for me. I didn't need the lecture on Central Figures or hierarchy or Cain/Abel relationships. I was convinced that God's plan for me was to go to school, no matter who my Central Figure was. I had thought it through while I was looking out that window of the vacant office building with the box of candy at my feet.

"Maybe I could live with my brother in Iowa City and go to school there. I'm sure I could get a grant. I could still be part of the CARP center there."

Paul looked at me with a half-smile, half-worried look, and then looked at his watch. "I have to go. I'll talk to Mr. Kamiyama," he said, and then ran off.

The next day a Japanese sister who had been part of the last blessing came to talk with me. She pleaded with me to just do what I was told. "You will be so happy when Father chooses a husband for you." She told me about how many times she was tempted to stray from God's path for her, but she stayed true and now she was a blessed couple.

When I stayed strong to my conviction, insisting that I knew God was on my side with this decision, her lecture became more judging, asking me how I could betray Father, when he needed everyone working on the front lines right now. I became silent. There was no use arguing. I had heard it all before and this time I was not going to budge. Finally she took my hands in hers and prayed for me.

"I know you will do the right thing," she said, as she walked away. I knew I would too. She just didn't understand me, or my relationship to God. I knew I was doing what God wanted me to do. There was no way I could give all I was capable of to the True Parents by selling candy every day. I could do so much more with an education.

I called my Mom and told her what I was planning. She was sure I could live with Ron. She said she would call him as soon as we hung up. "Just come home," she said. "We will work it out." She sounded like she was holding back tears. "Oh honey, I'm so happy."

When I called her back the next day, she said Ron and Roxie would love to have me come and live with them. They had recently become parents to a baby girl, Aarin, who I could take care of in exchange for living there. Ron had gone to medical school at the University of Iowa and was sure he could help me get enrolled there.

I found Paul and told him the news. He had talked to Mr. Kamiyama, who had spoken with the Japanese sister. I knew that at this point I was more of a problem than an asset in Mr. Kamiyama's eyes, after the way I dealt with Sharon and after my weeks of very low fundraising results. He clearly had no tolerance for members under his leadership who were not producing results. He had said I could go.

Paul cautioned me. "I can't help but worry, Diane. Satan will try everything to pull you into his world." We talked for a long time. He told me he would arrange for a bus ticket for me, and I was on a bus the next day. He gave me 200 dollars. "That's the best I could do," he said. "Call me if you change your mind."

CHAPTER 15

BEHIND BLUE EYES
The Who

M Y BROTHER RON AND HIS PARTNER Roxie welcomed me to their home and had a room set up for me when I arrived. Aarin was really cute; she was just a few months old. I felt like I didn't really know how to fit into their lives, but I was determined to make it work.

We lived in the country outside Iowa City on a 20-acre piece of land. The house was a 3,000 square foot log home. It was one of the bigger house plans for log homes available at the time and had a big loft for the master bedroom. There was an open bathroom with a big Jacuzzi tub looking out over the land. Throughout the house, open ceilings showed off the logs. There were three bedrooms on the main floor, plus a finished basement.

Within a couple of days, I went to the local CARP center. It wasn't anything like I had expected. I expected to be welcomed with open arms, but they were barely friendly towards me. It seemed like there was no one in charge and everyone was in a hurry. I talked to someone by the name of Kevin who was there between his classes, doing homework. He told me I should come to the next lecture; I don't think he knew what else to say. He had no frame of reference for the life I had led as a frontline member who had just come off the MFT. I thought about how it might feel for Vietnam vets to come home and talk to soldiers who had never been to war. I told him it was nice to meet him, but knew I would never fit in there.

I was able to get enrolled at the university because of my brother's connections. Once enrolled, I applied for grants and loans and signed up for required freshman classes.

On the first day of the term, as I went from class to class, I noticed a guy who was in all of my classes. We struck up a conversation on the way out of the classroom after the third class together and realized we were both on the way to yet another mutual class. As we walked together, he told me a little about himself and suggested we get together. We exchanged phone numbers and he said he would call me.

He called that night and we talked for a while and decided to get some pizza together the next evening. I could already see him as a member of the family. After classes the next day, we went out to a nearby pizza place. We discovered that we were born on the same day of the same year, within an hour of each other, within a hundred miles of each other. It seemed like destiny. I was sure God was somehow at work with our connection.

We did a few things together over the next couple of weeks, and each time I would tell him more about the Divine Principle. He wasn't as interested as I had thought he would be. He called one evening and when I started to talk about "the family," he said he really wasn't interested in hearing about it. The discussion ended with both of us knowing, without the words being said, that we wouldn't be spending any more time with each other.

I had a bedroom next to my baby niece's room and loved taking care of her. By the time she was learning to form words, we all agreed that her first word was Didi, an attempt at Diane. Roxie was an avid feminist and a vibrant, intelligent woman. I adored her. My brother was gone a lot, working the night shift at the hospital, so I spent most evenings with her. We had many long discussions about everything we could think of to talk about.

Roxie challenged me to think about things from a different perspective, but at the same time supported me in believing what I wanted to believe. It was winter and she would offer me glasses of cognac. She would warm a snifter and pour me a little and we would sit and talk by the wood stove. I hated it when my brother came home because our conversations would end.

I often felt restless. TV was especially annoying to me. I couldn't tolerate spending time without a specific purpose; it seemed like a waste of life. The constant sense of urgency I had become accustomed to was still running through my bloodstream without a clear direction.

We had weekly meetings to discuss household things like my schedule for taking care of my niece, how I would be getting to town for school, and who was doing what around the house. I felt bad when I had to be told that the garbage needed taking out when it was full, or that I should cook a meal once in awhile. It all seemed so trivial next to saving the world, and yet it became clear that I didn't have any basic living skills. I tried to fit into a lifestyle that felt completely foreign. After a couple of months, my chronic uneasiness seemed to subside a bit.

When Christmas came, my parents and sister came to Iowa City. I didn't feel like I knew them, nor had I much to say to any of them. Old feelings of resentment started to surface about how they had never really tried to understand what I had been doing. Everyone tried to act like we were close, but I felt very distant from them.

A few weeks later, over cognac, Roxie told me that my Mom had been trying to convince the rest of the family to have me deprogrammed for the past couple of years. The cognac caught on fire in my stomach with the news. I felt betrayed by everyone in my family except Roxie. She was suddenly elevated to true confidante status; the rest became completely untrustworthy. With this news, any walls that had begun to crumble regarding my belief of how Satan controlled my family were reinforced with new and stronger cement.

The one place I could connect with Ron was around music. He had a large record collection and a very nice stereo system. I hadn't listened to music in over four years. I listened to album after album, soaking the songs in like lotion on dry skin. Music and playing with Aarin made me feel most at home.

I began to hate the fact that I couldn't contribute to the household financially. I had no money for anything, and I didn't know what to do about it. I didn't want to ask my brother or Roxie for money and definitely didn't want to ask anyone else in the family. I contacted Lokesh and asked him what to do. I was surprised with how much he encouraged me to stay in school. He co-signed for a small loan through the school for me, which would pay for books and some things beyond what grant money would provide.

At this time, we had a strange meeting. Lokesh came to Iowa City, staying only for a day, and was negative about the church. He talked about going back to India to visit his family. I didn't know how to relate to him. He had been on such a high pedestal throughout my time with the Nebraska family, and had only grown in his grandeur while I was on the MFT under leaders that paled in comparison to him. He seemed less holy to me on this visit— charming and intelligent, but less like a leader or a man of God. He was also shorter than I remembered.

Roxie seemed to hit it off with him. They joked about him bringing her an elephant from India. She said she would keep it on the land.

The extra money from the loan helped. I made it through the winter term and earned good grades. In the spring, I took a philosophy course called The Pursuit of Happiness. The class started with reading Aristotle's *Ethics* and then juxtaposed that with other philosophers whose theories differed from his. I loved the class and the teacher. Unlike the rest of my classes, which were more formal and traditional, we sat in a circle. The class always included a lively discussion.

For the final assignment of the course, we were asked to write a paper entitled "The Pursuit of Happiness." It was to draw from our readings and discussions, but portray our own beliefs. I wrote a Divine Principle lecture.

After I turned it in, the teacher asked me to stop by her office; she wanted to talk to me. She wondered if I had misunderstood the assignment. She also had a box of clothes for me. She told me she had cleaned out her closet and had some nice things she was going to give to charity, but wondered if I wanted to have them. She told me I could rewrite the paper.

I took the clothes but it made me feel ashamed, like I must look bad or she wouldn't have offered them to me. I had no money for clothes. I got some things for Christmas, but I did tend to wear the same couple of outfits all the time. That's what I had done for the past four years and it was perfectly normal for the MFT.

I had no idea how to rewrite the paper. She had given me some advice on how to do it, but her words were a blur. I had been sure I had written an "A" paper, and that she would want to hear more about the Divine Principle after reading it. As I was going home that day, I suddenly felt I had made a terrible mistake. I had strayed from God and was getting further and further away.

When I got home I found Roxie in the garden, at the back of the house, with Aarin playing with some toys on a blanket. Roxie put me immediately to work helping her. She was wearing a straw hat and shorts with a shirt that looked like a bandana tied around her neck and her back. She was excited about the fact that she had bought 50 trees to line the lane leading from the road to the house. She wanted me to help her plant them. My worries about God disappeared for the moment. It felt so nice working in the garden with her, Aarin playing next to us. I decided to forget about the class and put school on hold for the summer.

I told Roxie about a job I saw advertised in the paper for a sales rep for a beer company. We laughed about how much sales experience I had. We walked around the house and she showed me the trees that had been delivered that day, pointing out where they would go, 25 on each side of the lane.

I got the job selling beer. It was a little distributorship owned by a German family who lived in the Amana Colonies. Hans, the owner, was friendly and had a German accent. His company had one sales rep working for it, and needed someone to take over because the rep was leaving the company. His name was Frank.

The company had a warehouse that sat by itself along a road outside of Amana. Frank took me inside and gave me a tour.

There were hundreds of cases of beer, and a forklift for loading the truck and moving the beer around. Frank showed me how to use the forklift and when to use a van, also parked in the warehouse, for small deliveries. There was a large refrigerated room for the kegs.

Frank was a nice guy and a close friend of the owner, but he needed a better job to support his family, he explained, while he poured me a beer from a small bar against a back wall with a keg hooked up for "tasting." His wife had just had a baby.

My job would be to call on the clients and deliver the beer. The beer was called Gemeinde Brau and was a recipe passed down through Hans's family. They also had the distributorship for Billy Beer, named after Billy Carter, the then-president's brother. Most people thought Billy Beer was the worst beer they had ever tasted, but people bought it anyway.

Frank taught me how to drive the truck. The key was staying as close to the middle line as possible without going over into the other lane. He told me not to worry about the other side while I was driving. It was always going to be all right on the other side if I stayed by the middle line. I drove with him until I felt comfortable. He went with me and introduced me to the owners of the bars and stores I would be calling on.

Since it was cheaper to buy 10 or 20 cases of beer instead of just a few, most people did, if they had the room to store it. Some of the bars needed the cases to be put into places like basements, which meant taking it down flights of old stairs. Frank taught me tricks about how to use the hand truck to get downstairs. I simply had to strap the beer onto the hand truck and ease it down in front of me. Kegs were awkward and heavy, however. He looked at me with some doubt as I struggled to get a keg out of the truck, but told me the owners of the bars would probably offer to help me.

That summer I delivered beer and helped Roxie plant trees. The owners of the distributorship invited Frank and a few of their friends and me over to their house one night for a game of pick the Gemeinde Brau. Everyone brought over a variety of kinds of beer to add to the collection that Hans already had waiting. We sat around and Hans would bring two small glasses of beer for each of us. We had to say which glass had Gemeinde Brau in it.

It was a strange setting. Hans and his wife had two severely disabled children. One son, who was a teenager at the time, was more functional than the oldest daughter. They also had another "normal" daughter between the two. The oldest daughter needed constant care and had to wear diapers and stay in a wheelchair. The son liked to sit in the car for hours. He came inside while I was there and he poured boxes of cereal out onto the floor, since Hans's wife had forgotten to lock one of the cupboards. She didn't seem upset, though. Hans's wife talked openly about it to me, explaining that the community was really supportive and everyone helped out.

After we drank quite a bit of beer, we ate cheese, crackers and fruit along with cut-up pieces of sausage and potato salad. There was also chocolate cake that was so moist and rich it had slight sag from its own weight. We stayed and talked until Hans felt like we were sober enough to drive.

I came home that night and parked the van, filled with beer, outside the house. I sat there and opened a can. A Bob Dylan song came on the radio, "Blowin' in the Wind." I turned off the radio when it ended and started to pray. I sat there for a long time, thinking about where I belonged and how I could use my life best for God.

I didn't sleep that night. I heard Mr. Sudo's voice. *We want to hug God, but we can't.* My breathing was shallow and I felt like a child who had broken my mom's favorite vase, and was hiding in the closet. I had betrayed God. Nothing else made any difference. I just had to get back to the path He had for me.

The next morning, I called Paul in New York and asked him if I could come back. He told me he would get me a ticket. His voice was consoling. I was sure I had made the right choice in calling him.

When I told Roxie, she wasn't as supportive as I thought she would be. She talked to me about finishing school, but I was beyond her persuasion. I called my Mom and told her about my decision.

"No Diane," her voice pleaded. She tried everything she could think of to talk me out of it, but my mind was made up.

A few hours later, Mom called back. She told me that she and Dad were going to drive to Iowa City the next day to see me. I was afraid she was going to bring deprogrammers with her, so I agreed to not leave before their visit if she promised to not bring deprogrammers. She agreed.

The next day, about an hour after Mom and Dad arrived, two deprogrammers appeared at the door. With this arrangement, Mom didn't "bring" them and besides, she said in her defense, they were just some girls who used to be in the group who wanted to talk with me.

One was about my age, maybe a few years older. Mom looked scared as she introduced us. "Honey, this is Elaine. She is an ex-Unification Church member." She was wearing jeans and a flannel shirt. The other one had been in some "Christian-based cult." She was dressed a little nicer and seemed less sure of herself, a little nervous. Elaine, however, seemed extremely confident. She had a kind of toughness about her, like she could be a high-school P.E. teacher.

"How much did you pay them?" I asked my Mom. I had heard about deprogrammers making lots of money off the families of Unification Church members. They were working directly for Satan, whether they understood it or not.

Elaine answered. "I just asked for a couple new pairs of jeans." I just stared at her. "All we want to do is talk," she said.

"There's nothing you can say to change my mind."

"Then why not talk to us?"

I stared at her for another minute, like a boxer staring at their opponent across the ring. I tried to size her up in an awkward silence and decided I could easily take her.

"Fine, but everyone else has to leave," I said. Roxie tried to say something to me but I interrupted her. "Just go, please." She had never seen me that angry and seemed taken aback by the tone of my voice. Mom started to tell me something about Elaine being a nice girl, but Roxie quickly stopped her and ushered her away, saving me from lashing out at my Mom. Dad was already outside.

First Meeting

Barrytown

Fight Song

Fundraising

Holiday on MFT

Moon at Prayer and Fast

Moon Estate

Moon's Limo

Prayer and Fast

Training 1

Training 2

Training 3

PART TWO

A NEW START

CHAPTER 16

LOSING MY RELIGION
R.E.M

BEFORE I WAS WILLING to give Elaine the time of day, I wanted some proof that she really was an ex-member. I questioned her about where she had joined, what missions she had been on, and asked her to give me the names of some of the members she had worked with. She convinced me, but I continued to look her in the eyes like an interrogator watching for signs of lying.

She had been a member for two years and had worked on Yankee Stadium. She could name some of the people I knew or at least knew of.

"I'm sorry you lost your faith," I told her. "Maybe I can help you come back." My sincerity to win her back matched her confidence that leaving was the right thing to do.

"I have a lot to go over with you. I brought some books and things—I'll be right back." She went outside and brought in two suitcases, then went back to get one more. She took the handle of the biggest one. "Can we go sit in there?" she asked, pointing to the living room.

"Sure," I said, curious about the contents she was lugging.

Marsha, the other deprogrammer, began to explain that she had been part of a small Christian cult. As she told her story, I became irritated listening to her. I wanted to tell her that I just wasn't interested, but instead prayed silently as if she wasn't talking.

I had her pegged as the high school cheerleader type. Her hair and make-up reminded me of a country singer, every hair in place and a bit overdone. She was soft-spoken and lacked Elaine's confidence. I also didn't see how what she went through had anything to do with my faith in the True Parents and the Divine Principle, which were about to be tested.

We went into the living room. Elaine opened up the suitcase. It was filled with books and papers and cassette tapes. She told me the reason she had left the group was that certain things turned out to not be true and that she wanted to talk with me about some of those things.

I was scared but didn't want it to show. I knew my faith was strong, but I knew Satan was strong as well. I felt like a pop quiz was about to take place that I hadn't studied for.

Elaine started with the Bible. She read scripture after scripture that contradicted the teaching of the Divine Principle. I wasn't concentrating. It reminded me of times when I had been fundraising and some Christian would try to get me to talk about scripture. I had never really cared about it. I knew there were brothers and sisters in the church who could speak that language, but I had never had the time or much interest in the Bible. The Messiah was on the earth and we were building the Kingdom of Heaven—that's what I cared about. People had been debating scripture long before either of us was born.

I wanted to call someone from the church who could respond to all of her contradictions. I was sure there were very good answers, from a Divine Principle point of view, to the points she was making. I began to feel frustrated and like I was failing the True Parents. Why hadn't I studied harder?

I had never become very good at defending the Principle against Christians who really knew the scriptures. It wasn't ever my mission. In fact, to do so as a member of the MFT was a way of letting Satan invade our mission. We were instructed not to have discussions about scripture or about anything that would slow down our work. My job was to bring in money to help Father do what he needed to do to build the Kingdom of Heaven. That rationale came back around in my mind over and over, but the louder voice kept asking why I hadn't studied harder. Now Satan was laughing at me.

I asked her if I could call someone. She asked, "Why should you have to call someone?" I hated her right then. "This is about you," she added. I kept thinking about the ticket to New York. When I get back to headquarters, I silently promised God, I would study harder. The more I made that silent promise, the stronger I felt.

Elaine went on for what seemed like hours. Roxie came in with some pizza and soft drinks. She asked me if I was all right. "I'm fine," I said with confidence. "We shouldn't be much longer." I just wanted to get it all over with so I could go to New York and ask Paul some of the questions that Elaine was asking me.

"I'll just play a tape of another ex-member for you while we eat." Elaine put a cassette into a player she had brought with her. It was harder to ignore what was being said on the tape than the academic arguments about doctrine Elaine had been making. This cassette was of a member explaining why he recently left. He talked about the process of opening his mind to some information that contracted the Divine Principle. I felt sorry for him at first, like he was a lost sheep, needing to be pulled back into the flock. Then, he started to talk about building a new life for himself—and he didn't sound very lost.

He said that as he began to open his mind to the possibility that just maybe he had been lied to, another thought began to take over. He started to realize that it was possible that he had just spent four years of his life working for a lie. That sentence made me lose my appetite. I put my pizza down.

I acted like nothing that was being said had any effect on me. He went on to talk about the time he spent looking at comparisons to other cults and seeing similarities. I stood up and went in the kitchen to get something to drink and to step away from what I was hearing for a minute. *My God, what if it's a lie*, I thought to myself, and begin to feel cold inside. When I went back into the living room, I asked if anyone was cold. They both said no. I grabbed a blanket off the couch and wrapped it around my shoulders.

The tape was over. Marsha said some things about her group, but I still didn't care what she had to say. Her words vaporized as she said them.

Elaine asked me if I wanted to take a break and go for a walk. I said no. She pulled out a huge book called *The Timetables of History*. She asked me if in my opinion the book was reputable. I assumed it was. It was a big book, hundreds of pages long with graphs and timetables throughout. I had never gone to college, but the book reminded me of a reference book I would probably see in a college library. She opened a Divine Principle book she had taken from her suitcase and started to point out specific dates in it. She would then go to the Timetables book and find the event. It was often off by many years. This became especially relevant when it had to do with exactly when the Messiah would be born.

I thought back to Lokesh's lecture, that night on the walk to Des Moines when I joined. The night I had realized everything in my life had been leading to my becoming a disciple of Christ. How could he have missed this? All those lectures, all those smart people, they couldn't all be wrong. There had to be an explanation.

"The whole theory that *supposedly* proves that Moon is the Messiah is based on how God has been working in exact numerology throughout history. If those dates are wrong, he can't be the Messiah…based on his own doctrine!" Elaine said this with her finger pointing to a date in the history book. She jabbed the book over and over with her pointer finger.

I was shivering. "I know there is an explanation. I really need to talk to someone who knows more than me about these things." Elaine just looked at me. I looked at her jeans and thought about her telling me that my Mom was buying her some new ones for doing this.

"Do you do this all the time?" I asked. I wanted to change the subject. I also really did wonder what her life was like. I was having a hard time thinking of her as Satanic; obviously she was really smart.

"No," she quickly answered. She told me she was in school and was studying history. "I'm just here because I had a few days between terms," she explained.

Marsha then said she came for the day just because she wanted to help out, if she could. I suddenly realized that when Elaine said she had a few days between terms, she meant she was staying here for a few days.

"I'm not leaving the family," I quickly said. "I just need to get some answers about the Bible and history for you so that you can come back." As I spoke the words, I knew Elaine would not be coming back to the family. Over and over I had heard that once someone leaves, it is rare that they come back. Satan's hold on them is too strong. "Let's get this over with. I'm not doing this for more than today," I announced.

I made myself a cup of tea and offered them tea as well. I started to warm up a little after my announcement that I was only doing this for the day. I felt better. They said no to the tea. Elaine was getting something else from her suitcase. We went back into the living room. She had a stack of papers. They were written testimonies of ex-members of different cults. She started reading them.

Marsha took a turn after awhile. I heard the testimonies of an ex-Hare Krishna and an ex-member of a Christian cult much like the one to which Marsha had belonged. There was also one from an ex-Scientologist. I felt sorry for the people who wrote the testimonies. I was sure Elaine was right; they were following a false Messiah or a cult leader. It was completely different from what I was doing, though. Moon was the real Messiah.

"So you agree these are cults," Elaine asked me.

"Yeah, I feel sorry for them," I said.

"I want to show you something." She went to get something else from the suitcase. I went to the dining room table and sat down.

Marsha was sitting with me. She made some small talk about the house and how she had never seen a log house as big. She was really trying to be nice, and it was a bit of a relief to talk about the house. I took her upstairs and showed her the loft. When we came back, Elaine had the book she wanted to show me and was sitting at the dining room table. We joined her. The sun was starting to set, and I wondered what everyone else was doing. I had heard the cars leave a couple of hours before.

Elaine showed me a book that she said was written in 1961 and had to do with brainwashing in China. She went on to say that what was interesting about it is that toward the end of the book there was a chapter that dealt with "ideological totalism." It outlined eight themes that are typically found in an environment that can control a person's decision-making processes. "It really defines brainwashing," she explained. "I would like to read the chapter and just see if you think these eight themes would describe the Unification Church or any of the other cults we have been talking about."

She read the introduction to the chapter. She stopped and re-read a couple of sentences. "But it is most likely to occur with those ideologies that are most sweeping in their content and most ambitious—or *messianic*—in their claims, whether religious, political, or scientific. And where totalism exists, a religion, a political movement, or even a scientific organization becomes little more than an exclusive cult."

She paused again and then read on. I started to feel cold again. The thought crossed my mind for the first time like a whisper I could barely hear: *What if he's not the Messiah?*

The introduction explained that there were certain conditions that were present in an environment where mind control was taking place. It also explained that those conditions affected people differently. Some people were more vulnerable than others to falling more deeply under mind control. Elaine stopped after reading the introduction and talked a little about her own experience. She seemed very sincere.

"The thing I liked most about being part of the group was the people." She looked almost sad when she said that, like she missed some of the members. She said that in her experience, the type of person who typically joined the Unification Church was idealistic and really wanted to do something to make the world better. She went on to say that a lot of people who join cults are at a vulnerable time in their life, like maybe they just broke up from a relationship or had been unhappy with school, or with their job.

I didn't say anything. I felt my teeth starting to chatter and knew it was from fear. The chapter began with a section on "milieu control." This was the first of the eight key aspects of mind control. It had to do with controlling as much as possible of what an individual sees, hears and experiences, but more importantly what goes on in the inner life of the individual. The "ultimate truth" is used to justify constant dominance or authority over the individual. The individual sometimes begins to share the "God's eye view" of the world. Autonomy is greatly threatened or lost. Elaine stopped again after this section.

"Does that sound familiar?" she asked. I didn't speak. I didn't even nod. I stared at her.

After a few silent moments, Elaine talked about her experience in the church and how after being in the group for awhile she began to question her views of the world and how she eventually would dismiss any of her opinions that disagreed with the teachings of the group as Satanic thoughts. She also talked about polarization between good and evil, which the book described. "Everything became either God or Satan," she said.

I thought about praying for Nixon and wanting to go to school instead of fundraising, but I didn't say anything that would let her know I was relating to what she was describing. I occasionally nodded in reluctant agreement when she asked me if I had experienced that kind of thing. She didn't push.

The next was "mystical manipulation." This had to do with using the idea of being "chosen" by a higher power, that the group or organization is being led by a mystical power. Everything can be justified with this argument. Elaine talked about a group called the Children of God that used this kind of argument to justify bringing recruits into the group through sex. They called themselves prostitutes for Jesus. I was glad we were talking about a different group: I could easily see how wrong and horrible that was. Then Elaine started to talk about how "heavenly deception" was used to sell products during fundraising.

I had used heavenly deception to justify countless actions during my years on fundraising teams. When we met up with teams from around the region for holidays, we would swap techniques for getting into places we knew we weren't supposed to be, or getting around rules or laws for God's benefit. I remembered sneaking into a drive-in theater, hiding in the back of the van so we only had to pay for two people to get in, then six of us jumped out with boxes of candy and began going car to car knocking on windows, raising money for "underprivileged children."

Again, the question ran through my mind: *What if he's not the Messiah?* It was now louder than a whisper in my mind.

The third section was called "the demand for purity." It had to do with the experiential world being divided into pure and impure and the demand that all impurities, especially within the individual, be sternly judged. I thought about Mr. Sudo's lectures when he talked about how beating your head against a wall if you have sexual thoughts was a good idea. The words in the book were academic, but I understood them as they described my world as a follower of True Parents.

The "cult of confession" was next. This had to do with the use of guilt and shame to control individuals. With each section, examples again flooded my mind. The fifth was the "sacred science," which was about an unquestionable doctrine. We definitely had that. Then it was "loading the language."

We were about to go over that section when Roxie walked in with Aarin to use the bathroom. She walked by the table and asked me how I was. I looked at her and the words, *What if he's not the Messiah?* were screaming in my mind so loudly that I began to hear the sound of glass breaking around me. I could hear it crashing down in a million pieces from every direction. Something was wrong inside my brain. I screamed. It was a wordless scream. I just screamed, covering my ears to stop the sound of the glass.

Roxie grabbed Aarin with the instinct of a mother protecting her child. The noise finally stopped. Roxie took Aarin from the room.

"Sorry," I said to everyone and no one, with tears welling in my eyes. I looked at Elaine. "Can we take a break?"

"Sure," she said. "Of course."

Roxie came back in the room and asked me what she could do. I told her I would be all right. She had taken Aarin to the bathroom and then come right back. I walked over to the living room and sat on the couch with the blanket wrapped around me. It felt like I had had a seizure. I told Roxie to go take care of Aarin. It was really important to me that she make sure Aarin was all right. I hated that I had scared her. Before leaving the room, Roxie came over and ran her hand gently over my hair, looked me in the eyes and told me she would check back with me in a little while. I appreciated that she was trying to help.

I couldn't explain what was going on for me in that moment, not even to Roxie. I didn't know myself. I felt like a hollow drum, completely void of everything. I asked Elaine if she could stay another day. "I can't talk anymore tonight," I told her. "I have a headache."

Marsha had to go. That was just as well. When Roxie came back, I asked her if she could ask Mom and Dad to go home. I definitely didn't want to talk with them right then. I wanted to go to sleep. I stared at the big book about timetables of history on the floor in front of me. "Please just let them know I'm not going back to New York," I said. I had no idea what was true except that I wasn't going back. The voice in my head had changed from *What if he's not the Messiah?* to *He's not the Messiah—he can't be.*

The timelines of history, the Bible contradictions, the ex-members' stories and finally the explanation of mind control and how it had happened to so many other people—how it had happened to me—were all bouncing around in my head like a bunch of superballs.

I cried strange, empty tears not associated with a pain I could physically feel. I was too numb. The numbness reminded me of how I felt after the rape. Still, the tears flowed and eventually I slept.

CHAPTER 17

IT'S TOO LATE
Carole King

ELAINE STAYED WITH ME for a couple of days. Before she left, I called Paul in New York and told him I wasn't coming back after all. The chilling fear I had experienced during the process of discovering that the Messiah was not on this earth had been replaced at first with emptiness, and then was replaced with relief, as the weight of a massive burden I had carried for the previous five years was removed.

I unashamedly told him I had talked to an ex-member and had decided that I couldn't be part of the "family" anymore. He was silent for several seconds before asking me to pray hard. He told me in a panicked voice I had never heard from him before that Satan had gotten through but that God wouldn't give up on me. The words were familiar, but they entered my brain this time through a new passage.

I liked Paul and felt his sincerity. The thought that I would never have to carry a case of candy from business to business again or repent for not wanting to do what my "captain" told me to do stood between his words and my heart. Nothing he said made me question my decision. There was no Messiah and I was not going back to that way of life. It was that simple in that moment.

Elaine and I talked late into the night the second night she stayed. I told her the story of leaving New York to go to school. I also told her about how I had started to feel like I didn't fit into the world I was living in now, going to school, which is why I had decided to go back to New York. I was worried that even though I felt clear about not wanting to go back to the Moonies, I wasn't sure I could stay where I was.

I didn't feel completely comfortable around Elaine. She seemed to look at life through her head more than her emotions. She was great at logic and it made me feel safe, but lonely. Her words were reassuring, but when our eyes met she didn't see the pain and panic I was feeling, nor did she acknowledge it in any way.

"You have it better than most people leaving a cult. You have had time away from the day-to-day lifestyle of the group. You should do much better at building a new life."

"I just can't believe all that was for a lie," I said several times as we talked.

Elaine told me a little about her life. She had a roommate who had an office job of some kind and they lived in a three-bedroom house, which they rented. Her roommate's sister had been living with them, but she recently moved in with her boyfriend. Elaine worked part-time at a bookstore, but was concentrating on school; she lit up when she talked about it.

She tried to help me think about what I would do. I didn't really want to go back to school, at least not yet. Going back to the little town I had grown up in was not an option at all. I had shut the door behind me when I left York, Nebraska, long ago.

Maybe it was pride, maybe just disconnection, but I did not want to be around my mom and dad or my brothers or sister. They seemed like strangers who could never understand what I was discussing with Elaine, what I was going through.

My mom and dad left to go home the same day that Elaine did. Before Mom left, she told me that an old boyfriend of mine had called, trying to find me. She gave me his phone number.

David was the only guy I had ever really cared about. I flashed back to a day when I was walking down the main street in my little town with a friend. David had moved to Colorado to go to school. I didn't even know he was in town visiting, and saw his car drive past me. There was a girl sitting next to him in the middle of the bench seat, where I used to sit. I later learned that they lived together, and had been together before he met me.

I lay awake that night remembering everything I could about David. The memories were like data passing by. No emotions were evoked. I wanted to feel something, but couldn't.

I called the number the next morning. His voice was familiar and I wanted to want to see him, but still felt an emotional void. He wanted me to come to Colorado to visit him and said that he would buy me a plane ticket to Denver. I agreed to go.

David was waiting for me when I got off the plane. It had been almost six years since seeing his face, and it stood out in the crowd. I went to him and he hugged me, smiling and looking rugged like the Marlboro man. His eyes smiled more than the rest of his face. He still had the same style mustache and the dot of facial hair in the middle of his chin, like Frank Zappa's, but smaller.

We stopped at a convenience store on the way to his apartment. He picked up a *National Enquirer*, among a few other items. He said he thought it was entertaining, which started a conversation about pop culture. He thought my opinion was a little drastic. It was hard to have a conversation about this, similar to the way it had been hard for me to write a paper for my philosophy class. The world was still black and white for me, with no shades of grey to complicate my mental vision. I wanted everything in the world to fit easily into good and bad, as it had when I was following the Messiah.

We arrived at his small apartment. He planned to take me to dinner. He told me I could sleep on the couch, but smiled a flirtatious smile that made me uncomfortable. In that moment, I wasn't sure why I had decided to come. I asked him about his family and he told me about his brother who lived up in the mountains. He wanted me to meet him. David liked to talk about his worldview. He was cynical and gave example after example of how stupid most everyone was.

We went to a restaurant that was unlike anywhere I had ever eaten. It was expensive and small and beautiful. I knew he was trying to impress me, and I was impressed—but I felt unsure how to behave. He ordered duck for me, which I had never eaten. We also had wine.

It seemed far too expensive for just one meal. For years I had been eating peanut butter sandwiches, and feeling guilty for spending money on a cheap honey bun pastry from a convenience store. Ron and Roxie ate mostly vegetarian food, often from the garden. I found myself judging him for living such a materialistic and shallow life, but continued to ask him questions that would keep him occupied talking about himself to fill the time.

When we got home, he invited me to sleep in his bed with him. He was funny and sexy and tried to get me to respond, but I couldn't. I was frozen; he would probably say frigid. We ended up talking about it. He explained that he needed to see what a woman was like in bed before he could consider a serious relationship with her.

Eventually he told me the truth about why he had wanted me to come for this visit. He had a girlfriend he was thinking of marrying. Before he could do that he wanted to see me, to make sure he was making the right decision. He wasn't pushy at all about the sex; he wanted me to want him. But, I just wanted to go to sleep… which we eventually did, without having sex.

As we drove into the mountains the next day, I had become a sounding board for him to talk about his girlfriend—what he liked about her, what he didn't. When we stopped by his brother's house, I was relieved to be around another person. His brother was funny and charming. He lived in a rundown shack of a house, but seemed happy and full of life. David obviously loved him, but told me all the things that were wrong with him as we drove back down the mountain.

Coming home after saying goodbye to David, the emptiness I had felt on greeting him turned to disgust. I knew David would marry his girlfriend now that he had crossed me off his list. He called a couple of weeks later and told me he had made that decision, and wouldn't be able to talk with me or see me anymore. I imagined him proposing to her over a duck dinner.

CHAPTER 18

I WANNA BE SEDATED
The Ramones

EILEEN CALLED TO CHECK UP ON ME a few days after I got back from Denver. She had talked with her roommate and wanted to offer me the extra room in the house they were renting. She invited me to come there for a few days to see the place and to look for a job, if I decided I wanted to move in.

I had purchased a '64 Dodge Dart for 400 dollars while I was working for the beer distributor. It was dented in the rear, but seemed to run all right. Its blue paint was faded, but it didn't look that bad to me; the interior was a bit worn, but the AM radio worked. I liked the idea that the engine was supposedly easy to repair if anything went wrong. It was a Slant-6, which meant nothing to me, but my brother said that was good. It also had a push button transmission, which was unique and fun to show people.

I threw some clothes in a suitcase and headed for Davenport, Iowa, which was about an hour's drive. I arrived at a little house in a neighborhood that looked like most of the people who lived there were elderly. Eileen's roommate, Melissa, got to live there for a really good price because her parents owned the house and rented it to them.

Elaine showed me the free room. It was empty, except for a mattress on the floor and a dresser. I figured that was all I would need. "It looks great," I told her.

Melissa was tall and thin with shoulder-length hair. She looked like a secretary to me, which, as it turned out, she was.

They were an odd pair. Eileen dressed in jeans and nondescript shirts; she seemed to live to study her schoolbooks. Melissa, on the other hand, seemed like she spent as much time reading fashion magazines as Eileen did history books. I decided to move in. They gave me a newspaper and I started circling ads for waitresses. I had decided that would be the best job for me to try to get. At least I would be around people; I felt lonely.

After applying to a few places, the manager at a steak house in a hotel in Rock Island, Illinois, across the Mississippi River from Davenport, told me he would give me a try if I would show up the following weekend. I would need a black skirt and white shirt. When I called and talked with Roxie, she suggested I come back that day and get some things. She thought she had some clothes she could give me for work. I missed her already. She had been my greatest supporter. Ron said all the right words and had let me stay there, but he either had no interest in really getting to know me, didn't know how, or both. I drove to Iowa City the next day. It felt good to be there, and I felt a bit lost going back to the apartment.

I caught on quickly at the restaurant, although there was a lot to learn. One of the waitresses, Becky, was really nice to me and helped when I was obviously overwhelmed. The restaurant had dark wood with white tablecloths and red and black accents. They were famous for their 22-ounce steak, which was meant to be shared.

After work, Becky invited me to go get a beer at a bar nearby. We went back over the river to Davenport to a place where students from the chiropractic college hung out. I started talking with a group of guys at a table next to us and ended up giving one of them my phone number. They were all students from the college.

The next day while I was driving to work, someone rear-ended me at a stoplight. He hit my car in the exact place the dent was, but assumed he had done it. The next day he called and offered me $400 to repair it—he didn't want to turn a claim in to his insurance. I calmly accepted, then started jumping up and down. Melissa had just come home from work for lunch. While I was telling her the story and how that was exactly what I had paid for the car, the phone rang again. It was Danny, who I had met the night before at the bar, calling to ask me out on a date. Things seemed to be working out.

For the next couple of months I worked evenings, went out drinking afterwards, and slept during the day. I hardly interacted with Eileen and Melissa at all. I started to hate waking up alone. I felt anxious, like I was doing something wrong or was supposed to be doing something else with my life.

One day when I woke up, I walked around the house. I went into Eileen's room. It was kind of a mess, with books scattered around and jeans thrown on a chair. There were pictures of her family in frames sitting on a dresser. Melissa's room was clean and orderly, decorated with matching curtains, bedspread and pillows. Her closet was stuffed with clothes on hangers and dozens of pairs of shoes. I went in the kitchen, where there was a newspaper open to a crossword puzzle half done and mail sitting on the counter addressed to Melissa. I went back to my room. There were no pictures, a few clothes and a mattress on the floor. There was a chair from the set in the dining room. I sat there for a long time. Empty.

I went out with Danny about once a week. He was recently divorced and had a little boy. He was clearly not over that relationship and talked about it a lot. He seemed depressed. There were several pictures of his son in his room. Danny lived in an old brick building that was part of student housing, next to the college. He ate at the cafeteria. We had sex a couple of times, but it was not fulfilling for me at all. He didn't seem to notice.

One day, I came to the building to see Danny and ran into one of his friends in the hallway. Danny was away for a few days. Rob, his friend, invited me into his room. He had some cocaine. I hadn't done any since before I joined the Moonies, and I decided to have some. We talked half the night and ended up having sex.

He made a big deal out of it, like we had something really special between us, but I didn't feel that way. I felt like it was something that had accidentally happened and wouldn't happen again.

He wanted me to tell Danny that we were together. I just wanted to get out of there. I had the next couple days off, so I drove to Iowa City.

I had some cassette tapes, made from some of my favorites from Ron's album collection, and the music helped relax the anxiety swimming through my blood. I practiced conversations I would have with Roxie, knowing she would help me sort out my confusion.

As I pulled into the lane leading to the house, I noticed several cars I didn't recognize. Some of Roxie's friends were apparently there, lesbians who worked with her at the women's clinic. I had met them briefly once before and Roxie had mentioned that information in passing.

In the Moonies, being gay or lesbian was the worst possible sin. Growing up in York, it was simply not spoken of, but I knew it was wrong for as long as I knew there was such a thing. I was very interested in them, however, and enjoyed watching them. They were confident and proud of who they were, and I felt something stirring in me, which I had been denying for years. I had pushed away intimate feelings toward Cheryl in York and Margaret in the Moonies. There were other women, as well, whom I thought of in that way. For the first time, I had a frame of reference for my feelings other than denial or Satan invading. I still couldn't tell anyone, however.

Roxie seemed worried about me when I told her about Danny and Rob. The conversations I imagined we would have were not happening. She was busy and short with me, taking a critical tone instead of the empathetic one I hoped for. Suddenly I felt like I needed to get out of town. While I was driving back to Davenport, tears cascaded down my cheeks.

I decided to go see Danny. Rob was in the parking lot behind the building and came to me when he saw me pull in. He approached me like we were war-torn lovers. I told him I was going to see Danny. It took him a little while to understand what I was saying. I didn't want to see him at all. I was upset and Danny seemed safer to be around than Rob.

"He doesn't want to see you," Rob told me. "He's my best friend. I told him about us. He seriously doesn't want to see you." He turned around to walk off, and then turned back. "Neither do I."

After work that night, my waitress buddy Becky invited me to come with her for a drink. Her boyfriend had just gotten a job bartending at a biker bar and she said he would give us free drinks. We sat at the bar and her boyfriend introduced me to a strong sweet drink that went down easy called a White Russian: vodka, Kahlua and cream. I drank enough of those that I shouldn't have gotten in my car, but I did. Becky stayed with her boyfriend. I immediately knew I shouldn't be driving and saw a motel, so I pulled in.

I remembered a trick I had learned in the Moonies. We would wait until someone was leaving in the morning and had left the door ajar, then go in and use the shower. In my drunken state, I thought I would be able to find a door partly open and go in to sleep for a while. I wandered around the halls and met a guy who was on the way to his room. I told him I was looking for a bed for a while. He offered me his. I took it.

I woke up a few hours later and crept out of the room, barely remembering how I got there. I went home and fell back to sleep on my mattress on the floor. When I got up, Eileen was sitting in the living room. She could tell something was wrong. She kept prying, asking me to sit on the couch and talk with her. The more she pushed, the more upset I got and shut down further into my fear. I wanted to tell her what was really on my mind, which was that I had come to realize I wanted to be with a woman, that I was empty and knew men would never make me happy, but I couldn't say the words. I didn't want to believe them, anyway. I just didn't know what to say, so I kept saying, I don't know. I was sure she thought I wanted to go back to the Moonies. I didn't. I told her I needed to do something different, but didn't know what, and started to cry.

After what seemed like hours, Eileen offered a suggestion. "I got a call from a woman in Minneapolis last week. She runs a house for people coming out of cults and wanted me to come there to work. I told her I couldn't because of school." She paused. "Maybe you should call her and see if she still needs help."

I called the Minneapolis woman the next day. She was friendly and upbeat, saying she was glad I called and that she really needed some help. When she asked me how old I was, and I told her 22, she hesitated for a second, but continued to make arrangements to give it a try.

CHAPTER 19

EVERYDAY PEOPLE
Sly and the Family Stone

I QUIT MY WAITRESS JOB over the phone and didn't say goodbye to anyone I had met, except my roommates. I just wanted to get away. Since I hardly had any possessions, I packed what I had and went to Iowa City to say my goodbyes to Ron and Roxie and Aarin.

I was excited for the first time in a long time. The plan was that I would work and sleep at the rehabilitation house four days straight, then be off work and go home to an apartment the next three days. Theresa, the woman who ran the house, said I could stay in an apartment with one of the other people who worked there for the first few weeks before I found my own place, just to make sure it was going to work out. It sounded good to me. The person with whom I would share the apartment would be working different shifts, so I would have the place to myself most of the time I was off work.

The Dodge just wasn't dependable enough to make it to Minnesota, so Ron helped me pick out a used car and get a loan for it. I traded in the Dart for a bright yellow '78 Toyota Corolla Sports Coupe. It had a cassette player in it, which alone made me love the car. I set off for Minnesota in my cool car with a box of tapes I had made from Ron's record collection. I was ready for a new life.

Debra, whom I had talked with on the phone, met me at the door when I arrived. I liked her immediately. She shook my hand, but and then, as I came in the door, she put her arm around my shoulders. "Let me show you around the place," she said. The rehab house was a suburban home. Debra and her two teenage daughters had bedrooms on the main floor. Two large rooms in the finished basement were set up with dorm-like furnishings. One room was for girls and one was for guys. Four single beds, one of which was a bunk bed, lined the walls in each. One male and one female staff were on duty at all times and slept in the rooms with the recently deprogrammed clients. The books on the shelves downstairs were available, and everyone was encouraged to read them. Some were about specific cults or cults in general; others were textbooks having to do with religion or psychology. There were also some random novels and a stack of board games. "Help yourself to these," Debra told me. "I always say, the more you read the better."

Upstairs, in the living room, the furniture was comfortable and homey and there was a TV. Debra didn't want it to be used unless there was something specific, like an educational show, to watch. The dining room and kitchen were where most activity took place. A large deck extended out past sliding doors from the dining room and led into a big backyard. Down the hall from the kitchen was a separate part of the house with three bedrooms. Debra's room was at the end, with her private bathroom attached, and there was a room for each of her daughters and another bathroom for them. That part of the house was off limits to everyone, except the three of them, unless by invitation.

I felt immediately at home and fell easily into the routine. Our job was primarily to simply be there. As staff, one of our most important tasks was to plan interesting things to do. Having fun was something I wasn't accustomed to, since during my years in the Moonies I had been made to feel that it was wrong to enjoy myself. The work was far too urgent and important. My job description for rehab required providing a light-hearted and relaxed atmosphere. This relieved me of the invisible censor I hadn't been able to shake, which had prevented me from enjoying pleasurable experiences.

At a staff meeting we talked about things to watch for, signs of a resident being in danger of going back to their cult. In social settings, severe and sudden feelings of confusion or cognitive dissonance could overwhelm someone who had recently made the decision to leave a cult. This was referred to as "floating," a term which was taken from a book that had just come out called *Snapping*, written specifically about the sudden personality changes that take place throughout a cult experience. Going back to the cult was a common occurrence when "floating" took place without the support of someone who understood what was going on for them. I knew that's what Eileen assumed was happening for me the day she told me about this job.

Part of the responsibility of a staff member was to watch for floating. We were always on the watch for signs that this was going on so we could help our clients through it. It was easy to spot: their eyes tended to glaze over and they seemed nervous, like they needed to go somewhere and were late. When we saw signs of floating, it was simply a matter of providing them with information to help them make sense of their confusion.

I understood it completely. It was like what happened to me after talking to the teacher of my philosophy class, before I decided to go back to New York. Something just snapped in my head and all I could feel was guilt for not being a better disciple of the True Parents. I just knew I had to go back and repent for my sins.

Other times, after my deprogramming, I found it hard to concentrate and would drift off into feeling confused and numb. The simplest of decisions were really hard. Much of the time, I felt like an alien from another planet.

Even though I was being paid and trained as part of the staff, I knew I was not so different from the people whose families were paying for them to be there. I soaked up the information offered, and was happier and less anxious than I had been in a very long time.

We went to concerts, shopping, dance clubs and tourist attractions. One of my favorite activities was going tubing on the Apple River. We would drive to a place called the Apple River

Hideaway. There was a shuttle bus and inner tube rentals available. We came equipped with a cooler full of beer and would rent inner tubes, one for each of us and one for the cooler. The shuttle would take us to the drop-off location and we would step into the river, tie our inner tubes together and float for hours. One of the staff members gave me a t-shirt with the words Apple River Junkie on the front.

There was something about spending the day floating down a scenic river with nothing to do but talk, laugh, and occasionally throw an empty beer can at one of the targets set up for that purpose along the river that soothed me. I had been saving the world for years, but meanwhile I had forgotten there was such a thing as relaxing in the beauty of nature.

The staff consisted of all ex-cult members, except one woman whose brother had been in a cult. She had just graduated with a psychology degree. Her name was Shari and she was my favorite. We teased each other often and had long talks about everything from how it was going with her boyfriend to what it was like growing up in Nebraska, and I knew she always had my back.

The rehabbers, as we referred to them, were constantly changing. There were deprogrammings happening in various parts of the country on a regular basis that could result in bringing us a new person. At the same time, others were ready to leave and move on with their lives. Staff members didn't stay long either, I discovered. The job seemed to be a stepping-stone in the lives of ex-cult members.

It was fascinating to meet people coming from various cults and learn what life was like for them. There was a guy who came through who had been in Hare Krishna. He still held firmly to some of the beliefs. One belief he liked to talk about was how men were superior to women. He was about my age, tall and lanky with deep acne scars.

From the beginning, his arrogance and the pleasure he got from making comments about male superiority made me dislike him. In fact, I couldn't stand him. When my blood started to boil from being around him, Shari calmed me down. He did open up to one of the male staff members, and talked about his parents' divorce and how much he resented both of them. When I heard that, I could empathize more with him. Unfortunately, he left in the middle of the night and went back to Hare Krishna. No one was ever held at the house against his or her will, but participants had to agree to the rules of the house, which included not leaving the house alone. He left through a window while we were all sleeping.

Most of the people who came through were in their early 20s. We sat in a circle in the living room to talk once a week. It was casual, but everyone was required to attend. Sometimes it took up most of the day. I found the conversations interesting, and they added structure to the week. We talked about what we were doing the upcoming week, who wanted to come to different events we had planned, and most importantly, we talked about how everyone was doing.

One girl, Karen, came to the house from COG—Children of God. I had never heard of them, but quickly learned a lot about the group. The first thing Debra did when Karen got there was to arrange for her to be tested for STDs. The group was famous for using the female members to bring new recruits into the group through a process called "flirty fishing." Another term was "hookers for Jesus." Sex was used as a way to open up possible recruits to better receive God's love. It was considered an altruistic act, and not intended for pleasure. I remembered my deprogramming and how we had talked about this group.

Karen didn't go out much with us. She did lots of reading and met with a Christian counselor several times. Before we had our meetings, she would pray silently. She was soft-spoken and had a wide smile that wasn't shared very often, though by the time she left we got to see it more. She played the piano really well. I heard she took it up more seriously when she went home. Debra got letters from the "kids" who came through the house quite often, and she always lit up when she read them. She was always so happy to hear they were doing all right. She really did think of them as her kids.

Another interesting cult was the Brethren, also referred to as the "garbage eaters." Mark, the guy who came to the house from that group, had been living with the Brethren for over two years. His family had been looking for him the entire time, hiring a private investigator, who finally tracked him down. This group gave up all material things as well as all ties to family and friends to live nomadically with their new brothers and sisters. The United States was known as Babylon, and all who were not members were considered sinful. They survived by looking through grocery store dumpsters for old produce or anything they could find.

Taught to have little communication with anyone outside the group except to proselytize, their key mission and the only reason to speak with anyone, Mark was reclusive at first. He came to the Apple River with us one time and I floated down the river in a tube next to him. We ended up laughing a lot and he talked about going back to college when he got home.

There were a number of Moonies who came through the house and we always had a special bond, comparing who we knew in the group and what missions we had been on.

Debra was really good at making everyone feel at home, but also making sure everyone was getting what he or she needed. She spent many nights sitting at the dining room table talking with whoever pulled up a chair. Often it was about what they were going to do with their lives when they got back. The conversation would turn to how they felt about different things going on in the world, but I noticed she never pushed any belief on anyone. She was like a favorite aunt who just cared about whoever wanted to talk to her.

During our meetings, tears arrived from unexpected places. With some encouragement from Debra, an ex-Moonie named Sheila talked about an experience she had the day before. She had volunteered to talk with a group of clergy about her experience. That was not unusual; I had done that several times with various groups from churches or schools. But as she was speaking to the group, she suddenly burst into hysterical tears. Debra was there for her, fortunately. Somehow, in the moment of telling her story, she had been overcome with the weight of what had happened to her.

It seemed like everyone in the circle that day completely understood. I certainly did. As she was talking, I remembered a similar experience that had happened to me just a few weeks prior.

One day, on my day off, I went in a public bathroom at a fast food place and saw someone my age putting on lipstick. Unexpectedly, a lump rose in my throat and I had to go into the stall and cry. I couldn't stop the tears for what seemed like an abnormal amount of time—so long that I got scared something was wrong with me. In seeing that young woman precisely applying her lipstick, I realized that I couldn't remember what it was like to put on make-up. It was considered Satanic to care about looking good in the cult and I had avoided make-up, even after my decision to leave the cult, telling myself I preferred the "natural look."

As I listened to Sheila and remembered my own breakdown, I empathized with her sudden onset of pain, her moment of realization that the story she was telling wasn't fiction or someone else's life. It was hers, it was mine, and it was all of ours sitting in that circle, whose minds had been raped and who would need to occasionally fall apart.

During nice weather we often had a barbeque after our meeting day to lighten the mood. It was all right to have a beer or two, but not to get drunk. Debra had a strict rule of no drugs or sex while staying at the house, along with the minimal drinking rule. There were occasional jalapeño eating contests or water balloon fights and inevitably there was flirting here and there. Board games were encouraged as good mental exercise. There wasn't too much idle time, however, with all the planned activities. The TV was rarely on. People staying in the home could sleep as late as they wanted. Everyone was on their own for breakfast and lunch, but Debra always made dinner.

Different types of one-on-one counseling were available to everyone, and counseling was encouraged. Some met with a rabbi or a priest, for instance, or a licensed therapist. It seemed like there was a run of people from little Christian-based groups for awhile. They all wanted to go over the meaning of scriptures. I avoided those conversations.

Chapter 20

Secret Agent Man
Johnny Rivers

O
NE DAY DEBRA ASKED ME if I would be interested in helping
out on a deprogramming. The client was a Moonie, and there
was no one on the team who was from that group. She assured me
that I wouldn't need to do much of the deprogramming work; I
would be there to catch the person trying to lie about what being a
Moonie was like. I decided to do it.

I set off for Bloomington, Indiana with Ed and Rich, two
other staff members who were on the case. We flew into India-
napolis and rented a car, then drove to Bloomington and waited
for the word to go to the designated place where the deprogramming was to take place.

Ed called Debra from a pay phone. She was helping coor-
dinate the logistics and hadn't heard from the family yet, so we
decided to go to the campus and walk around to kill time.

While there, Ed happened to see a posting stapled to a bulletin board. The heading read: KIDNAPPERS AT LARGE. He grabbed
it and showed us. David, the Moonie we were there to deprogram,
had apparently found out what was going on and had reported to
the police that a kidnapping had been planned. We quickly found
a pay phone and called Debra. She told us to get out of town. We
drove away and Rich started to worry about the rental car.

"What if someone checks rental car records and the cops
spot our plates?" Rich was Irish. He had red hair and freckles.

Usually he was upbeat and quick to make a joke, but at that moment he was dead serious and scared. Ed tried to calm him down.

"We could throw mud on the plates to cover the numbers up," Rich suggested. We pulled over on a tree-lined farm road off the highway and tried to put mud on the plates to hide the numbers, but I thought it just looked stupid, since the rest of the car was clean. Still, we got back on the highway with our muddy plates.

"I'll ride up front if you want to sleep," I told Rich. He had mentioned while we were on campus that he had hardly slept the night before and needed a nap. He took me up on it, fortunately. He was making me nervous.

About an hour out of town, we got a flat tire. When we looked in the trunk, there was a donut tire there in case of an emergency. Half the size of a real tire, it was meant to get you, slowly, to a tire store. With the sunlight gone, we had to change it in the dark. Rich started to joke about it by the time we were back on the road. I was relieved to see his smile. We drove to the closest town, left the car behind and found a Greyhound bus station, which is how we got home.

By the time we got back, Debra had gotten word that the police weren't even looking for us, since David had just posted the notices. Because nothing had taken place and the family had denied planning to hold him against his will, there was no crime. David's sister, who was against the deprogramming, had told David about the plan and ruined the chance for their parents to set it in motion.

We told and retold the story sitting around the dining room table with Debra, laughing at the events of our escapade: muddy license plates, flat tire, and the smelly guy on the bus who sat next to Rich. But it was sobering when the phone rang and Debra had to comfort David's parents, who felt they had now pushed their son deeper into the cult. This was probably true.

Most of the rehabbers came to the house from deprogrammings; Debra had nothing to do with those. There were teams of deprogrammers across the country that knew of the house and recommended it to the families with whom they worked. Sometimes these teams needed help on a case they were planning, and since they knew Debra's staff was mostly ex-cult members, they often made requests for us to get involved. Ed went out on cases fairly regularly.

I started to go along every chance I could. The approach to deprogramming varied with the people I accompanied, but not by much. There was always a need for someone to be present that was from the client's cult, if at all possible. In all the cases I went out on, it was simply a process of providing information, and talking. The cult members were lied to and taken advantage of by their various groups, through the use of mental manipulation. Once they began to consider the possibility that maybe it was all a lie, the structure began to crumble. At that point the family, with whatever help we could provide, could begin the process of helping them rebuild their lives.

The pay was by the day, and varied, often depending on what the families could afford. It was never much, though, considering the risks and the 24-hour nature of the job. Travel and food were taken care of by the families.

CHAPTER 21

I'm Coming Out
Diana Ross

A DESPERATE FATHER came to Debra one day asking for her help. His daughter, Linda, had joined a relatively small, fundamentalist Christian-based group. Linda was turning 18 in a couple of weeks, so her parents could still legally go get her, but they had to act fast and they knew they needed help.

Linda had moved into a house with some people from the church. She had turned her back on her family and friends for this new life. She had given up the music she loved along with her jeans; now she wore skirts and tied her hair back in a bun. "This is not my Linda," the father kept saying, as if she were an impostor.

We talked over the details of the situation and decided on a plan. A group of us, along with the police, went to get Linda. The police knocked on the door and explained why we were there. Linda came out of the back of the house and saw her Dad, along with the police and the rest of us standing in the living room. She looked scared, but came with us with little resistance. She had her head down, praying, as we left the house.

It was a four-hour drive back to Debra's house. There were two cars, and I wasn't in the same car as Linda. She rode in a car with the other deprogrammers, one of whom had been in a similar group. By the time we got to Debra's, Linda not only agreed that she was better off leaving the group, she also couldn't wait to get back into her jeans.

I liked Linda right away. She was so excited to be free of that group. They had convinced her that God was working through the leader of the group, and that she had been full of sin for liking the things she liked. At first she was happy to be included in the "family"—but it was really hard for her to follow all the strict rules. The more I was around her, the more I could see why she had a hard time with them.

Since she had only been involved in the group for a few months, she didn't suffer from the kind of mental damage that some of us had, who had been in groups for much longer.

Linda's personality pulled me into a level of carefree abandon that I hadn't known since I used to giggle with my best friend, Kim, in seventh grade. We were at a store one day and one of her favorite songs came on the speaker. She grabbed my arm. "Don't you just love this song?" she said, and sat down right in the middle of the cereal aisle, cross-legged, eyes closed, head moving back and forth until it was over.

After being at the house for a few weeks, she asked Debra if she could join the staff. My roommate was moving out, so she moved in with me. We became close friends quickly. We both had dreams of traveling the world and made plans to do that together, spending hours looking at world maps, deciding on routes. Our decisions about where to go were based on things like lyrics to songs we both liked. For instance, there was a Bob Dylan song with a line about Tangier. We had to go there for sure. Debra just rolled her eyes, shook her head and walked away when she heard us planning.

Even though Linda and I worked different shifts, our hours overlapped occasionally and we always enjoyed our time together. Linda's spontaneity and enthusiasm for little things touched a part of me I had stifled for so long it felt almost foreign, like feeling sunlight after being trapped for years in a cave. Even though I loved the bright world of playing with her, I found I quickly ran for the darker shade of our serious work, deprogramming, and trying to decide what to do with my life after small doses of Linda.

Sometimes we would smoke a little pot together. Linda would laugh and laugh and then make something to eat. It didn't matter what it was, it was always delicious. One day, she took some crackers and put ketchup and cheese and oregano on them and put them in the oven. I was in the other room and she yelled for me like there was an emergency. "You have to taste these!" I ran into the kitchen. She was so happy and proud of herself. The weight of the world disappeared when I ate her cracker pizza and she told me about her friends in Oregon I had to meet, and then jumped to telling me about some funny thing that happened to her when she was seven. "Why are these soooo good?!" She said this mid-sentence, grabbing another cracker and laughing.

Moving back and forth from floating off into her childlike freedom to putting her feet back on the ground, and trying to keep her on track as we planned our cross-country trip, was an ongoing dance. We had given Debra notice and started getting rid of the few large belongings we had accumulated, mostly from garage sales. We had to make everything we needed fit into my car. We agreed that the things we mostly needed were some clothes, a cooler for food, and lots of cassette tapes. We pointed the car west, turned up the music and hit the road.

Other than a couple of stops along the way to visit my family, we drove straight through with our sights set on the Pacific Ocean, stopping only to sleep in the car when we got tired.

ONE DAY WHEN LINDA was driving, I was staring out the window thinking about some women we had just seen at a truck stop where we stopped for something to eat. They were obviously lesbians. Linda knew something was wrong and kept asking me what I was thinking about. Finally, when we stopped at a rest stop and decided to go for a little walk to stretch, I told her I thought I was a lesbian.

The words didn't come out easy. I stumbled and stammered around until she finally said, "Just say it." I sat down and cried. She told me she loved me and would be with me if she wasn't into guys. When we stood up she linked arms with me. I started to cry again. She lovingly called me a crybaby, and offered me a crumpled up Kleenex from her pocket as we headed back to the car.

It was a warm day when we took our shoes off and ran to the salty, chilly ocean. Standing with the waves gently slapping my legs and breathing in the ocean breeze, I knew I had to make my home near the coast.

We spent some time in California walking on the beach and exploring the sights and sounds, then headed to Oregon where we would stay for a few days with a friend of Linda's. I found Oregon to be even more beautiful than California and started making plans to live there.

I checked in with my Mom when we got to Portland, and she told me someone had been trying to get ahold of me about a deprogramming. I called the number she gave me and within a few days was on my way to Canada.

Chapter 22

Midnight Rider
The Allman Brothers

ALTHOUGH I HAD HEARD THEIR NAMES, I had never worked with this team of deprogrammers before. By the time I arrived, Cindy's deprogramming had already been underway for a couple of days. When I came in the room and the team introduced me to her, she seemed relieved I was there.

Cindy had been in the Moonies. She hadn't seen her family the entire time and had finally been given permission to come home for her uncle's funeral. After the funeral, she thought she was going to see her cousin's new house, but instead was taken to another location where her deprogramming was to take place.

Joe and Charlie, the other deprogrammers, left the room at one point and I was alone with Cindy. We had been talking about fundraising when they walked out the door to take a break. It was a relatively low-key conversation at that point, but as soon as we were alone she changed the subject abruptly.

"Please don't let them rape me," she pleaded. She was trembling and her eyes were tearing up.

"What? I asked. "You think they would do that?"

I went over and sat next to her on the floor where she was sitting on a big pillow. "Cindy, I promise, no one is going to hurt you." I paused and went on. "That's just something being spread around in the Moonies to make you afraid to listen to what we're saying." Her face was starting to get calmer as I sat there with her.

"Seriously, all we want to do is talk with you." She started to cry, and then she started to sob. I knew it was sinking in. Her world, her Messiah, it was all crumbling. I just sat there with her. We didn't speak for a long time. I handed her a tissue.

By the time we finished that case, there was another being planned. I went back to Oregon and within a week was headed to the Florida everglades. We waited with family members for word that Kevin, the young man we would be deprogramming, was in the "safe house." It was late evening when we headed down a dark road through a swampy area where they joked about alligators. I wasn't amused.

As we were getting out of the car, a tall skinny guy came running toward us. "He just went out the bathroom window," he said. Everyone jumped out of the car and started looking around the area. I went in the house, however; there was no way I was going anywhere near those alligators.

Soon Charley came and got me. "We need to get out of here. His family's going to stay and look for him, but we should go, and fast." I knew exactly what Charley was thinking; even though it was Kevin's family stopping him from leaving, what we were doing could potentially be described as kidnapping. We got in the car and went back to the house, hoping to hear we could proceed with the deprogramming. However, we ended up going home, never meeting Kevin.

When I got back to Oregon, Linda had decided to go to school in Albany, at a local community college. She asked me to stay and be her roommate. I decided to give school a try, as well. We moved into a little apartment not far from the campus, but since Linda loved being in the country, we kept looking for something outside of town. Eventually, we found a little A-frame house for rent out in a rural setting off a road that led through a mountain pass on the way from Albany to the beach.

I signed up for classes and started feeling like I might do all right in school this time. Money was running out fast, however. My only source of income was from deprogramming. Several times there were plans in the making for me to leave on a case, but they would fall apart or get delayed, and I was broke. I would lie awake worrying. When I did go on cases, I would have to try to figure out how to get through my classes without getting really behind.

It was a long drive to school from our new place. Even when I wasn't gone on a deprogramming, I sometimes missed classes because it didn't seem worth it to drive in for one class on a Tuesday morning, especially when I hadn't slept well the night before. I dropped classes regularly. Anxiety became my constant companion—unlike Linda, who seemed to be fine. The things that upset me didn't bother her. She dropped classes sometimes too, but it seemed okay to her; she just joked that it might take her 10 years to get an undergraduate degree. To me, everything felt like a crisis.

My stomach started to bother me. I would get sharp pains that sometimes doubled me over. At night, my stomach would make loud noises. One morning I woke and the pain was so bad I could barely stand up. Linda took me to an emergency room in Albany. They gave me something for the pain and cramping and told me to see my regular doctor the next day. Not only did I not have a regular doctor, I also had no insurance or money. Besides, the pills they had given me made me feel better.

But I couldn't stop worrying. My thoughts would go from money to school to feeling like something bad had happened, but I wasn't sure what. I kept feeling like I was in trouble. The stomach problems returned, but this time there was also blood in my stool. I went to a doctor. He wanted to run a panel of tests, but that would cost much more money than I had. The other alternative was to try some things and see if one would work. If they didn't, he said, the tests would have to be done. He put me on a strict diet, told me to take antacid—lots of it—and to do whatever I could to get rid of the stress in my life.

My mom seemed to be calling a lot during that time. She couldn't understand why I had to live so far away. When I talked to her about the stomach problems, she really wanted me to come home. Soon, I saw it was better to downplay my medical problems with her. She did send some money, though, and it helped to ease the stress a little.

The term had just ended and I decided to get a job and work for a while, since school was more than I could handle right then. I heard about a job in a cherry-canning factory that paid a decent amount, so I decided to do it. I lasted three days. My job was to pick rotten cherries or leaves or sticks out of the fruit going by me on a conveyor belt. The work was loud and we were required to wear earplugs. After a couple of hours, a loud bell would ring, the belt would stop and we could go sit in a dirty room with a soda machine and some tables and chairs. Some of the people went outside to smoke. Most of the workers spoke Spanish, so I sat by myself outside. The bell would ring again and back we would go until lunch, the afternoon break, and finally the end of the day.

The second day, I came equipped. I had made a list of things to think about and songs to sing to myself while I stood there. During break I asked around about how long people had been working there and how they stood it. Some had been there for years; I couldn't believe it. This part of the work was seasonal, so they said they did other things, like worked in the groves sometimes, but I was told I would have to work the "belts" for at least one full season before I could do other things. I overheard a conversation in the break room. One of the girls who had worked there for several years was really excited because she was going to be trained to drive a forklift to load pallets on and off trucks.

Driving home from the cannery I remembered selling candy in a factory and how certain I was that my life was exactly where it was supposed to be. I was a soldier of God and all history would remember me as a disciple of the second coming of the Lord. I felt scared that I would never feel that certain about my life again. I quit the next day.

Linda and I decided to move to Portland, and after a lot of looking around, we rented a tiny house outside of the city. It was nestled in a beautiful setting in the country with a filbert orchard on one side and a field of concord grapes on the other. We could have all the grapes we wanted. They were doing some things to repair the house, however, and we had some time before we could move in. Linda decided to go back to the east coast for awhile to visit her family.

Linda's friends let me stay with them until the house was ready, and while there, a deprogramming case came up that really excited me. It was in Ireland, and I would be working with two of my favorite deprogrammers. I got everything ready to go to Ireland.

CHAPTER 23

WHEN IRISH EYES
ARE SMILING
Roger Whittaker

I FLEW INTO SAN FRANCISCO and met up with Scott and Shari before we caught our flight to Dublin. The client was a Moonie named Conor who had been in the group for seven years, and had recently been matched to be married. We would be meeting family members and driving to Galway. Conor was already with his family, visiting for the first time in five years.

It was a big plane and a long trip. Scott was sitting in a different section than I, and found me a couple hours into the flight to show me a story in an Irish newspaper he happened to be reading. There was a young schoolteacher named Lauren who had been on a vacation to America and had met and joined the Moonies. Her family had friends in America who had organized protests outside the San Francisco Moonie house and were demanding that Lauren go home.

Scott left me the paper and went back to his seat to try to sleep. I read the article and glanced through the rest of the paper, then tried to get some sleep myself. That was hard to do, after reading the article about Lauren. I was excited about going to Ireland, but the thoughts keeping my mind from resting were about Conor and Lauren. I knew Conor's family was desperate to help him get out of the group and hoped we would be successful. I also wondered what Lauren's family would do if she came back. She would need some support and some information. I finally dozed off.

Conor's Uncle Peter met us at the airport and told us it would take several hours to drive to Galway. I was tired of traveling and not looking forward to another long trip, but the countryside was beautiful. It reminded me of Oregon with all the lush green, but the stone walls and old buildings—along with the fact that we were driving on the left side of the road—constantly reminded me how far I was from home. Scott asked lots of questions about the castles and history of the places we were passing. I mostly listened to Peter's accent, which I loved.

When we arrived at Peter's house, his wife Carolyn made us some tea. Scott offered to go with Peter to the house we would be using for the deprogramming, so they could discuss some of the logistics. There was no reason for us all to go, Scott said. Shari said she needed to lie down for a little while. I was tired, but restless. Carolyn asked me to walk with her to go pick up a couple of items from the market. As we walked, she kept trying to talk with me about politics in Ireland and asked me questions about how Americans felt about Ireland and the conflicts going on there. I knew absolutely nothing about it and kept trying to change the subject by asking about Conor. This lack of information about the world in which I lived was often a source of embarrassment for me. It was as if I had been in a coma for five years.

We arrived at the "safe house" after Conor had been taken there and had been told what was happening. He thought he was going to be visiting a niece. The house was small, with two bedrooms, a small kitchen, a living room and one bathroom. The furnace burned peat, and it heated water that ran through the house. Conor was in one of the bedrooms waiting to talk with us in private, while family members or friends of the family took turns sitting around in the living room, in case Conor decided to bolt. He had been made aware they were there for that purpose.

The first day, he was understandably angry and defensive, but by the second day he was starting to be interested in what we had to say, to his own surprise. His process reminded me of my own.

In most cases it takes several days, or more, for a person who is controlled by the kind of mental manipulation that Conor experienced to get to the point where he is sincerely interested in what is being presented. In Conor's case, as in mine, part of the invisible chains holding us captive had already grown weak.

We took turns being in the room with him, sharing information and talking. I was alone with Conor reading an article to him on our third day when Scott interrupted and asked if he could speak with me. Shari came in and took over the reading, and I left the room.

"Remember that article in the newspaper I showed you on the plane?" he began. "Well, the family of that girl, Lauren, found out we're here and wants us to deprogram her, too."

"When?" I asked.

"Now!" Scott was sweating. "Can you turn this heat down?" he asked Conor's cousin. Potatoes were cooking on the stove in a pressure cooker next to where we were standing. We stepped outside the back door to get some air.

He explained what he knew. Lauren, the girl in the newspaper article, had been sent home by the Moonies to stop the bad publicity. She had only been with the group a couple of weeks, but the family was worried about her going back. "I don't know how word got out that we were here, but they talked to Conor's family and asked if we could help them."

Conor's father came outside to talk with us. Scott and Shari had already discussed it. "We thought we could put her in the other bedroom and not tell Conor she was there," Scott said. "I just think it would be a bad idea for them to have any contact." I agreed that if we did decide to do this there should be no contact.

"How's he doing?" asked Conor's Dad.

"Really good," we both said in unison. And he was. Conor had started to ask questions about the information we were presenting, and on several occasions that morning had asked to see something again that we had read earlier. He was starting to relax and even joke around a little with us.

One of the reasons I liked working with Scott was that he had such a comprehensive collection of information that he brought with him. Between the three of us, we had just about everything I had ever seen on mind control, and stacks of articles about various cults, as well as tapes and written documents of ex-members telling their stories of what life was like in their cult. We also had the entire collection of *Master Speaks*, as well as a Divine Principle book and various other texts only Moonies would have.

Conor's family decided they were willing to allow Lauren to be brought to the house, as long as we felt it could be done without being detrimental to Conor's process. We all agreed to move forward with the plan, since Conor was doing so well. Shari was in the room with Conor. Scott and I discussed the possibility of one of us going along with Conor's dad to meet up with Lauren and her family, so we could begin talking with her during the ride back to the house. I volunteered. After driving for what seemed like a long time, we pulled over along the road and a limo pulled up behind us. I felt like I was in some spy movie. Lauren was ushered to our car, got in along with her mother, and we took off. She didn't speak the entire time back to the house, although we tried on several occasions to engage her.

Lauren's mother sat in the front seat. She also said very little, except to make the point that Lauren knew we were ex-members and that she had reluctantly agreed to talk with us. After explaining this to us, the mother stared out the window for the rest of the drive.

Lauren's mother escorted her into the second bedroom. Scott, Shari and I moved back and forth between the rooms. Neither had any idea there was another deprogramming going on just a few feet away. By the fifth day with Conor, which was the second day with Lauren, they were both doing really well.

Conor had decided not to go back and seemed relieved that he could leave the group. He had really started to open up with us about what life had been like for him. He was unhappy in the Moonies and had been for some time, but was enduring it because he believed in the True Parents. A wife had been chosen for him to whom he was not the least bit attracted. He had been having a very hard time staying motivated and inspired for the past couple of years. I understood and related to his story. I told him so, and he asked to hear about my experience. I told him about Galveston, where my struggle to fundraise began. How my inability to produce the results at fundraising evolved into not being able to do it at all, and eventually to knowing I had to go back to school. He was empathetic and said he was happy for me that I was able to finally leave.

Lauren had not been involved long enough to know many details about the group. She was shocked to learn a lot of what we explained to her. We would read something from a speech Moon had given and she would say, "You're kidding me. Let me see that." She would read it for herself and shake her head in disbelief.

We were tired but feeling good about how things were progressing—and then there was a knock on the door. It was the police. Somehow, the Irish Unification Church had tracked us down and called the police to report a kidnapping. We figure they must have followed one of Conor's family members from his parent's house.

The police were really nice. They talked with both Conor's dad and Lauren's mom and were clearly understanding and supportive. They didn't want to be there, but said they had to talk with both Conor and Lauren. We had no choice. They waited by the door while we went in and explained the situation to each of them.

They came out of their rooms, were introduced to each other, then to the police. We were confident about the work we had accomplished, but it was still early in our process, and we knew our clients could go either way. First Conor and then Lauren each told the police they weren't being held against their will. The police apologized for bothering us, and promptly asked the Moonies waiting outside the house to leave.

Scott was standing next to me. "I thought for sure I was going to wet my pants," he said, breaking the silence and dissolving the tension into laughter.

We spent the rest of the day in the living room talking, and then decided to go to Donegal, where Lauren was from. Her family had a house in the country that would have more room. We drove there and spent the evening eating, singing and talking. The house was amazing; it was over 400 years old. Lauren played the guitar and they sang Irish songs about the war, the sadness of brother against brother, and songs about the beauty of Ireland. Unfortunately none of the three of us were good at singing, so we couldn't contribute much.

We left Donegal and Lauren's family the next morning and went back to Galway, stopping for a walk on the beach. At one point Conor took off running ahead of us. We all looked at each other, knowing none of us could come close to being as fast a runner as he. "Get him, Scott," I said, tongue in cheek. Scott, a big guy, was already out of breath from our walk thus far. He leaned on a rock.

We watched Conor get farther and farther away. Finally, we saw him stop and sit on the sand. Eventually we caught up with him and sat down next to him.

"How you doing?" Shari asked.

"I'm free," he said. "I'm free!"

That night there was a feast at Conor's house after which we went to a pub nearby. Everyone kept commenting on how Irish I looked with my red hair and skin tone. I do have Irish blood, and looking around I could see why they thought so. The pub was like I had imagined it would be. It was an old stone building with a red door. There were men in tweed caps holding pints of Guinness, and every now and then someone would break into song and the people around them would join in, swinging their pints to the beat of the song.

We were sad to have to leave the next day and vowed to come back for a visit.

CHAPTER 24

YOU CAN'T ALWAYS GET WHAT YOU WANT

The Rolling Stones

W HEN I GOT BACK I started looking through the want ads for work. Deprogramming was exciting, but I needed something more…normal. While driving home one day, I saw a *help wanted* sign in the window of a restaurant, so I went in. A woman who reminded me of my aunt Hazel greeted me and told me to sit anywhere. She was a big woman with red hair and deep dimples, like Hazel's. I told her I was wondering about the job opening. She served the table she was heading for when I came in, then went back to the kitchen. When she came back she handed me an application form to complete. I sat at the counter and started filling it out with my name and address and phone number. Then, it asked for my employment history and education.

I stopped writing. I felt nervous, like I was hiding the fact that I was an alien from Mars. I tried to think if there was anything I could write, but after a few minutes, I asked if I could take it with me and bring it back later. That was fine, the woman said. I threw the application in a nearby trash can, and drove to a newspaper stand to buy the daily paper. I went back home to search for other jobs, hoping I wouldn't have to share anything about my past. I simply didn't have a past that anyone would understand.

After mulling over whether there was anything I had experience doing, I decided to look for a sales job, since that's what I had done so successfully during my years in the Moonies… sort of. There was one ad that said no experience needed. It turned out to be selling storm windows and heat pumps. The guy who talked to me when I showed up at the office was a 40-something Italian guy. I told him I didn't have any experience but was sure I could do it. He said that's what counted, and told me to come back the next day to go through a couple days of training, and then I could go with him on some sales calls to learn the ropes.

I went through their training and became an appointment setter. It was supposed to lead to making lots of money. That was an epiphany to me—to think of making lots of money. Right then I decided lots of money was the thing I needed to be happy. I was told that anyone could get rich doing this if they worked hard enough, so I started planning what my life would be like when I became rich.

It didn't work out quite as planned. The guy who hired me started coming on to me and I quit, but I had seen another ad for one of their competitors and decided to call them. I talked to a woman there who decided to give me a chance. I would be working with her part-time, but not for a couple of weeks. In the meantime, I went to interview for a waitress job. It would be in the evenings, so I thought that could work out well. I could do both.

The manager of the restaurant was the owner's daughter. It was a family-owned Italian restaurant, famous for their pizzas. She didn't make me fill out an application form. Instead, she just talked to me. I decided to be honest with her about my background. She asked me the typical questions I get from someone who finds the story interesting. How did you get into that? What was it like? How did you get out? After I'd answered her questions she said, "I like you," and gave me the job.

The house in the country was finally ready to be occupied, and Linda was due back in a few weeks. I started going to garage sales to buy things for the house. At one of the sales, I bought a bed. The woman I bought it from was charming and seemed a bit flirtatious. She offered to bring it to me. The next day she came to the house, as promised, with the bed. She was very friendly and asked me what I did for fun. "Not much," I said, meaning it. She wrote down her name and phone number and said maybe we could go out dancing sometime. I assumed she was a lesbian and had just asked me out, but I wasn't completely sure. I hid the paper away.

I started working at the restaurant. The girl that was training me was about my age and I liked her right away. As I was pouring a pitcher of beer for one of my tables, I told her I was only there temporarily. "I'm going to be rich soon. I sell heat pumps and storm windows," I told her. My conviction to make money was a replacement for the conviction I had to save the world.

She didn't miss a beat. "I'm stickin' by you, then," she said. She didn't seem to be joking. I certainly wasn't. We became fast friends.

Linda came back but only stayed for a few months. She had decided to go to school back where she grew up. It was a fun summer. The owner of the little house we occupied told us we could sell the grapes if we wanted to and could keep whatever profits we made. He even brought us a scale to weigh the grapes, and helped us with the u-pick signs. He was an old guy who liked having us there. We gave him a beer whenever he stopped by, and he joked about having to sneak it so his wife wouldn't know.

I kept getting called for deprogrammings. Donna, the manager of the restaurant, was very understanding and let me go whenever one came up. I hadn't been doing well at the storm window job. The woman who hired me told me in a condescending voice that I was just a little too young. And then she fired me.

I was called about a case in California, where I went with a couple of other deprogrammers, but we never got to do the case. Our target, Carl, had cut off all ties with his family, so the only way a deprogramming could happen was for us to do a "snatch." His family hadn't heard from him for over two years, and they were more nervous than any relatives I had been around. Just the idea that they would finally get to see their son was enough to make them anxious, but in this case he would have to be physically grabbed off the street and taken to a safe

house. Unfortunately, he must have been moved from the location where he had been spotted just a few weeks prior. After a
week of waiting for an opportunity to grab him, the case was
called off.

Carl's parents, Claire and Jeff, were part of a support system for parents with children in cults. Someone in the group,
whose daughter had recently joined the Moonies, tipped Jeff off
about Carl's whereabouts. The girl's family had been invited to
the Moonie house for a lecture and was introduced to the members living there. Her dad tried to remember everyone's name and
wrote the names down when he got outside, to share with other
parents in the support group. One of the names was Carl. He fit
the description his parents provided, so his family began to plan
his deprogramming.

When Jeff and Claire, who hired us for this job, got the information about where their son was located, they sent a detective
to watch the house and make certain he was there before they
hired a team of people to help them. According to the detective,
it was definitely Carl. He had been seen several times coming and
going, so they went forward with the plan.

Most deprogrammers, including me, never got involved until
the person was secured in a safe house. Immediate family members had to be present at all times and insure that the cult member
was not allowed to leave the house. So as usual, we stayed nearby
waiting for word that Carl was in the safe house and that it was
time to see him. In this case, unfortunately, that time never came.
The family was heartbroken.

That was the second case in a row that had failed. The month
before, I had gone to Illinois with Joe and Charley on a case that
had come to nothing. We were in a farmhouse and the girl was
especially angry about being there. Her family seemed to have
problems beyond the fact that Shelly—the girl we were there to
deprogram—was in a cult. The parents were divorced and clearly
didn't get along. Shelly's brother seemed to be the one who was in
charge and who cared about Shelly the most. Some of his friends
acted as "security" and took turns watching the door.

After the first day, Shelly was still not talking with us or eating. When we would try to read something she would pray out loud, referring to us in her prayers as Satan's disciples.

We were all physically and emotionally exhausted at the end of that day; we had come straight to the house from the airport. Shortly after we arrived, Shelly grabbed a pen and tried to jab herself with it. This was one of the recent techniques the Moonies had been taught: if they could get to an emergency room, they could tell the doctors they were being held against their will.

We had taken everything out of the bathroom she could possibly use to hurt herself, including taking the mirror off the wall. Usually, someone goes in with the person, but she said she had to "take a dump," so we stood by the door. The lock had been removed. All of a sudden, we heard a loud noise and tried to open the door. She had taken the lid off the toilet and wedged it into the door so it wouldn't open. She was climbing out a window behind the shower that somehow we hadn't even noticed was there. Everyone ran around the house, and through the fields that surrounded the house, but there was no sign of Shelly. We gathered our things and left right away. We wondered what her family would do if they did catch her—carry her back screaming?

I decided to take a break from deprogramming after those two cases and was happy to return to my little house in the lush Oregon countryside.

We harvested grapes that summer and made juice with a juicer that our buddy, the owner of the property, had lent us. We also sold quite a few grapes with our little u-pick business. When the filberts were ready, a helicopter flew low over the trees and blew them down, and then a big vacuum kind of machine came through the rows and picked up the nuts. There were a lot left, however, and we had garbage bags full of the leftovers. Our families received nuts and juice for Christmas that year.

It was becoming clearer, as months went by, that Linda wasn't happy in Oregon and wanted to move home to the east coast, which she eventually did. Alone and restless, I tried having sex with a guy, just as a test. He was a friend and knew I thought of myself as a lesbian, even though I wasn't with anyone at the time. After that night with him, I knew for sure that I wanted to be with a woman. It wasn't that sex with him was horrible, and it wasn't about him. I just knew.

I called the number on the piece of paper I had stuck away months ago from the woman who delivered the bed. She remembered me.

CHAPTER 25

WALKING ON BROKEN GLASS
Annie Lennox

WITH LINDA GONE, I decided to move into the city. I had quit my job working at the Italian restaurant and got a job at a tavern in a part of Portland known for its bohemian feel. There were lots of artists, musicians and people living alternative lifestyles. The bar I worked in had live jazz on the weekends. It was a tavern, serving mostly beer and some wine. The food menu's highlight was the bacon burger.

I usually worked the floor, taking orders from the tables and mostly bringing them more beer. Eventually I started working behind the bar and in the kitchen. On slow nights, I did it all. That was when the regulars came in and hung out for hours. I got to know them and started pouring their beer as they walked in the door. I worked late and slept through the mornings.

Cheryl, the woman who had delivered my bed, was definitely a lesbian and introduced me to what it was like to be part of the gay community in Portland. We went on a few dates, but she wasn't over the woman she had most recently been dating and they ended up back together. I began to accept the fact that I was gay, but kept it from my family.

Linda had introduced me to one of her friends, Kayla, who happened to be a lesbian and had a lesbian sister. I looked her up after Linda left. Kayla lived in a big house with her partner and their daughter by the river, not far from where I worked. I stayed there with them for a few months and then unexpectedly they split up, and both moved out. I decided to take over the house and quickly got several roommates. I barely knew any of them. Kayla's sister lived in Washington State. Her girlfriend, Tracy, was moving to Portland for a job and needed a place to live, so she moved in. Tracy suggested two other women, whom she'd known from when she was in school. They moved in as well. Our schedules were all different, so we didn't often see each other.

Tracy and I started going out to bars dancing or to play pool. I had a crush on her and we messed around a few times, but mostly just had fun going out. She was an artist. I admired her work, and she had lots of energy, which I enjoyed. Her hair was always a little tousled and she dressed like she had just rolled out of bed. Somehow it worked, however. She could get away with a lot because of her charm and quick wit—and her beautiful blue eyes.

Whenever I was with her, or with my other roommates, I felt like I was young and unburdened. Then I would get a deprogramming call and be yanked back to the reality of where I had been. Talking with my Mom and Dad on the phone left me feeling like I didn't belong anywhere. I was sure they wouldn't understand my being a lesbian, and I didn't plan to tell them.

One night I came home late after closing the bar and there were fire trucks outside the house. One of my roommates had set a few pairs of wet shoes by the woodstove that had caught on fire while she slept. Fortunately, another roommate smelled smoke and acted quickly. I was worried about what the owners of the house would do, and I had to leave the next day for a deprogramming.

This client was voluntary. It was so much nicer to talk with someone who wanted to talk with us. The family was in Idaho and their daughter had walked away from Scientology, but was considering going back. There was an ex-Scientologist on the case who did most of the talking. I was just there to draw a comparison to how cults in general work. At first she dismissed me entirely, saying that of course the Moonies were a cult, but that Scientology was really different.

Being in a more passive role than I usually played gave me the chance to experience the deprogramming process a little differently. I knew some things about Scientology but had never heard about the doctrine in such detail. I caught myself wanting to laugh at the doctrine, especially the really far-fetched things that were like science fiction but even less sensible, things that only members who were in the innermost circles knew.

During a break, I went for a walk with the ex-Scientologist, Garrett, who was the primary deprogrammer. He was tall and skinny and wore thick glasses. He reminded me of a kid down the street from me when I was in seventh grade in Nebraska who was the smartest student in my grade, but was considered a nerd. I asked him more about the teachings and joked with him about which one of us believed the most far-fetched doctrine. At first, we each defended our group as the most logical, but toward the end of our walk we were laughing and trying to outdo the other with ridiculous things we had believed.

There was this teaching called the "Wall of Fire," which was written by L. Ron Hubbard, supposedly under the influence of alcohol and a variety of pills. It is a part of Scientology teaching that has to do with extraterrestrial civilizations and alien interventions in earthly events, collectively described as *space opera*.

"Okay, so let me get this right, Garrett," I said to him. "In another galaxy far, far away, some guy named Xenu froze a bunch of people, who just happened to look like us, dress like us and even drive cars like ours, and Xenu put them in boxes around volcanoes on earth and detonated bombs inside the volcanoes to take care of overpopulation in his galaxy?"

He didn't skip a beat, cocked his head and said "Let *me* get *this* right . . . Eve had sex with an angel, then seduced Adam. This tragedy caused all suffering in the world since the beginning of time and finally God sent Sun Myung Moon to end all suffering. The fact that he is a crook and ends up in prison for tax evasion is justifiable because"—he paused for emphasis—"well, it's really not necessary to understand because mere mortals can't understand how God works. You're right," Garrett said teasingly, "talking snakes and a crook for a savior makes a lot more sense."

"Yeah, I guess you have a point," I conceded.

It was a sunny day and I was glad I had come and had made a new friend. He was a little nerdy, but I liked him a lot. We stopped at a corner store and bought some drinks, before heading back into the house. We called our sparring contest a tie and toasted with our sodas.

The next day, there was a psychologist working with us on the case who talked about how the brain will find a way to make illogical things seem acceptable because of the discomfort of cognitive dissonance. That made a lot of sense to me and I smiled across the room at Garrett. I talked about some of the more farfetched beliefs I had held, but in this setting, unlike on the walk the day before, it wasn't funny at all. I started to tear up a little as it all came home for me, once again—what I had been through and how much it still hurt.

The girl we were talking to met my eyes in their vulnerability, and I saw her "get it." After that moment, she no longer dismissed me as being different than her.

I left the case thinking I would try to just do voluntary cases from then on. It was so nice to not have to worry about if the person would try to escape.

The day I returned home, Tracy met me at the door as she was heading out. "Bad news, she said. We have been evicted." The owners of the house needed to do repairs from the fire and had decided to sell the place, so we had to move out. One of the women didn't have money to pay me the last month's rent, so she gave me her bicycle as payment.

Tracy and I rented an apartment. Her girlfriend, Sheila, would be moving in with us in a couple of months.

One slow night at my job, a guy came into the tavern and sat at the bar. He talked to me about his job. He worked for *The Oregonian*, Oregon's major newspaper. He had people working for him that managed teams of teenagers who would go door to door getting people to subscribe to the paper.

"Do they make much money?" I asked.

"If they work at it, yeah, they can make good money," he said. "Some of my people have several teams and they do really well. Why, you interested?"

It sounded like being a team leader on the MFT, only a lot easier. It seemed like something for which I actually had valid qualifications. He gave me a business card and told me to call him. I was sick of bartending and knew I had to find a way to get rich; otherwise I would never be happy. This could be a start.

I quit my job at the tavern and started working with a team of kids selling newspaper subscriptions. I couldn't fit very many into my little car, but I would drop a few off, then go get others and drop them off, then go back and check on the first group. Sometimes, Tracy came along and helped. She was always looking for a few extra dollars and I could make more with her help, so it worked out. I was starting to build a small circle of casual friends in the lesbian community and enjoying living with Tracy. Our little place seemed more comfortable to me than that big house with roommates I hardly knew.

I got a call from my parents one day saying they were coming to Oregon to visit me. They had a travel trailer and had decided to make Oregon one of their stops. I was not looking forward to the visit; I no longer knew how to relate to them. I felt like I was living a secret life they would find repulsive and wrong, and once again it seemed like I was doomed to never fit into my own family.

They weren't sure exactly when they would arrive, and when they did, some of Tracy's friends from college were visiting. Our apartment was messy from partying. Her friends had slept on the couch and floor so there were blankets in piles and a pizza box along with bags of chips on the table. I had at least gathered up the beer bottles, but the air had that stale after-party smell. On top of the mess, there wasn't much room on the street for their big fifth-wheel trailer.

They asked me to come to the beach with them "so we could have some nice time together." I could see the disapproval on Mom's face when she looked around the apartment. Dad seemed more worried about his trailer than the apartment, but I could also tell he really wanted some time with me. There was something in his eyes when he said we could play cards in the trailer—a soft begging I couldn't refuse.

I agreed, but drove my car instead of riding with them so they could keep going down the coastline from there. I talked Tracy into coming along. Her friends had just left and she had a couple of days open with no plans. We played cards with Mom and Dad in the trailer that night. They said we could sleep in the trailer with them, that there was plenty of room, but we wanted to sleep on the beach. We took a bunch of blankets and found a place on the other side of some sand dunes from where they parked the trailer.

I wanted to talk to Tracy about how I was feeling so distant from them but she didn't seem in the mood for that kind of talk. She really wasn't someone I could open up to like that. Instead, we had sex. As I lay there while she slept, I realized there was no one I could talk to like that.

Tracy and I went back to Portland the next day. We looked at a map with Mom and Dad as they made their plans to head down the coastline. I was relieved when we said goodbye. I wanted them to go before they got a closer look at my life.

Sheila moved into our apartment the following month, and it felt awkward. I tried to stay away as much as possible. One night, I went to a bar to play pool with some women I had met there before. I offered them a ride home afterwards. We came to an intersection with no stop signs, and I didn't stop. Neither did the car coming from the other direction. The car crashed into the side of my car. I had been drinking, but not very much. Police showed up and had me walk a straight line and touch my nose. The cop who tested me decided I was all right, or maybe he just felt sorry for me. I was really upset. One woman's foot was hurt pretty badly; my car was small and she was in the back seat. Her foot had been partially under the front seat at the time of the crash and got stuck under there. They had to use some tools to get it out. I watched in tears as the ambulance took her to the hospital. She spent some time on crutches, but recovered quickly. That was the only injury. My car, however, was totaled. I didn't have insurance, which was against the law, so my license was revoked. And I lost my job, since it couldn't be done without a car.

The day after the accident, Tracy and Sheila were both out of the apartment. I was alone and couldn't stop crying. I knew I needed help, but wasn't sure where to turn. I picked up the phone book and started calling social services places. I just needed some help getting back on my feet, I kept telling people who answered. But every call was a dead end. I would make a call, hang up the phone, and cry; then once I felt I could talk again I would try a different number, only to be told I didn't qualify for their program.

"Maybe you should go to a hospital to be evaluated," a woman from a help line suggested. I just hung up and cried some more. I wasn't going to some psych ward.

I pulled myself together when Tracy and Sheila came home late that night. Unbeknownst to me, someone had told Sheila there was something going on between Tracy and me. Sheila often lost her temper and was typically overly dramatic; I had heard about this from both Tracy and Kayla.

Sheila started yelling at us. Then she went into the kitchen and got a butcher knife and came out with it. Tracy quickly calmed her down and took it from her, but something in me snapped.

I remembered the bike that my former roommate gave me when she couldn't pay her rent. I got it and took off out the door. Outside it was dark and pouring rain. The image of the guy at the dump with the brick over my head was stuck in my brain. I drove around, going nowhere in particular, all night. Several hours later I was wet, cold and numb. As the sun was coming up, I found myself near the house of some women I had recently met. I didn't know them well, but I knew their names were Deana and Misty and that I had enjoyed meeting them. I sat on their porch until one of them came out and found me there.

They were different than most of the women I knew, a little older and more mature. One of them, Deana, had run a shelter for battered women in California before they moved to Oregon.

They invited me in and made me breakfast. I told them my story. Misty was very sweet and wanted to make sure I had enough to eat. Deana wanted to help me find a place to live.

I couldn't stay with them, but they suggested that I call a women's shelter. I was, after all, escaping domestic violence. I called the number they gave me. It was a bit of a stretch, but the woman who did the intake with me let me stay. She also put me in touch with a therapist, who was willing to see clients from the shelter on a sliding scale. Her sliding scale started at almost nothing, which was just over what I had, but she agreed to see me and I managed to come up with the token amount she was charging.

CHAPTER 26

ONCE IN A LIFETIME
Talking Heads

WHEN I MET ANDREA, my therapist, I immediately liked her. Her office was in an old house that had been converted to professional spaces. It felt safe and comfortable.

I had figured out ahead of time what I needed from her. I calculated that I needed one or two sessions for the current situation I was in, a couple of sessions for unresolved cult issues, and I could probably use another one or two for the rape. Since I considered myself a cult expert, I planned to offer her some sort of trade: In exchange for some of the therapy, I assumed I could teach her something about cults.

When I explained my plan to her regarding what I would need, she suggested that maybe we should not set limits on how much time it would take. She asked me to begin by telling her a little more about what was going on for me. It was surprising how fast the 50 minutes went by. By the fourth or fifth session, I began to see the value of having someone with whom I could speak. I started seeing her once a week, sometimes twice a week. I never did mention my idea for the trade.

I stayed in the shelter for a couple of weeks. Fortunately, Deana and Misty had just come across a house they wanted to rent that was much bigger than the one they were in. They would need a roommate to make it work and asked me if I wanted to move in with them. I borrowed some money from my brother to help with the deposit and to pay my part of the rent. It was horrible having to ask him, but I didn't see any other way. I hadn't been called for a deprogramming in months, but started making calls to see if anyone needed help on a case. I had to find something to do to make money. I could use public transportation, but at some point wanted to have a car again.

I got a job telemarketing, knowing it was only temporary, until I could get my license back. I really needed a car, however, and a friend sold me hers by letting me take over the payments.

Just as one part of my life would begin to stabilize, someone would come along and draw me into their whirlpool of need. I was a magnet for people who would take advantage of whatever they could get from me. I had several short sexual relationships during that time, but quickly ended them. One was with a woman who ended up in jail for drugs; another was with a woman who was verbally abusive to me. The only one who was stable was already in a relationship, and she eventually cut me out of her life.

My sessions with Andrea were a mix of problem-solving my latest dramas and crises while trying to work on deeper issues that were causing my instability, as well as my broken family relationships.

I had a new scheme that was going to get me rich every few weeks. At one point, I considered becoming a surrogate mother. I went as far as going into an agency and signing up. I got a call that there was a couple that wanted to use me. At the last minute Andrea helped me realize that it was likely I would have a hard time handing over the baby.

Jobs weren't working out. I thought about going back to school, but it seemed more important to make money. Somehow, I came across a program that was funded by grants. Its purpose was to create jobs for unskilled workers by training them in the field of sales and helping them get hired into positions. I signed up and got a certificate in sales techniques. I was a star student and had an offer before I graduated. The job was selling memberships to a campground system for people with RVs.

People who owned RVs would get an offer in the mail telling them they had won a prize, and to claim it they just had to go on a tour of one of our resorts. I was taught how to take them on a tour of the resort and then go through a sales pitch that would make them want to be a member of the system. When I had finished the tour I called in the "closer" to clinch the deal.

I made what seemed like a lot of money within a few months. At first, I bought into the idea that what we were selling was a great thing, and then as time went by I began to see that it was a bit of a con. I was talking people into something they couldn't really afford and that they would probably regret buying later. I decided to quit. About that time, Deana and Misty broke up and Misty moved out. We could no longer keep the house, so I had to get an apartment by myself.

I kept seeing Andrea. Like the Peanuts character Pig-Pen, I walked around in my life surrounded by a cloud of emotional dust. Andrea consistently tried to clear it away so I could see myself without the cloud. Week after week, we tried to sort out and understand my unhealthy patterns.

After quitting the RV membership job, I was back to one get-rich scheme after another. The apartment I was in didn't work out. I moved again, after only a few months, to a different apartment. I found the cheapest place possible, since I wasn't making much money.

I started dating a woman named Paula. She was just ending a marriage and had taken over the house they were buying. The house was comfortable and nicely decorated. Paula's life seemed safe and well grounded. We went to the beach, on hikes, and to movies. Her roots gave me something to hang onto during the storm of my life.

After a little more than a year of seeing Andrea once or twice a week, the cloud started to lift. There had been many tearful sessions examining what I had been through. Telling the story of the rape was particularly painful, since I had never spoken of it outside the cult, and only then with Lokesh.

Glimpses of hope that I could mend the relationships with my family began to appear in my vision for the future. I could see myself clearing the air and no longer carrying, as Pig-Pen claimed he did, the dust of ancient civilizations. I could finally let go of the message carved deep within me of being Satan's spiritual mother. Even though on the surface I could laugh at the notion, something deeper held me responsible for saving the world.

After living on my own long enough to know I didn't like it, Paula's roommate situation changed and we decided to try living together. My plan was to look for a more stable job, not in sales.

CHAPTER 27

THE HEAT IS ON
Glenn Frey

I HADN'T FOUND A JOB YET and got a call from my friend and
fellow deprogrammer, Scott. There was a family from Sweden
whose daughter, Beatrice, was a Moonie living at the center in
Colorado. Arrangements had been made to pick her up the following week. Even though I had made up my mind to quit deprogramming, except for voluntary cases, I decided to go on this one
last case. I needed the money and they needed my help.

It was nice to be working with Scott again. We went over the
details of the plan with the family that was hosting us, the detectives and Beatrice's family. It seemed like the logistics were thor-
oughly planned and that the safe house would be comfortable and
well suited to our needs. It was in the country and was fairly new
and big. The finished basement was set up for the deprogramming. There were plenty of people ready to help watch Beatrice
and take care of things like cooking. There was also lots of food.

Detectives had been hired who had a plan to pick up Beatrice.
They had been doing surveillance on her for days and had been waiting for the right moment to bring her to the house. The plan was to
physically take her off the street. Her parents would be in the van so
that she would know right away she was safe. She would be driven to
a remote location, where another vehicle would be waiting to transfer
her—just to be safe, in case someone saw the "snatch." Only then,
would she be brought to us. All bases were covered.

We waited for several days. Suddenly there was a whirlwind of events. Beatrice arrived and we took her downstairs, where we planned to begin the deprogramming process. She refused to talk or eat, which was normal during the first day or so of a deprogramming. During any deprogramming, we always encouraged sleep and eating healthy food, since we wanted the clients' brains to function optimally. We also wanted clients to feel as safe as possible—to know their families would be there with them and that no one would hurt them. We always made it clear that we simply wanted to talk to them and that their families had been worried about them. Often, the first day or two was all about making our clients feel as safe as possible.

Unfortunately, before we had the chance to begin the process of trying to make Beatrice feel safe, we got word that someone had seen her being forced into the van. That person followed the van to the second vehicle and called the police. A friend of the detective who had been doing surveillance had connections in the police department. He called and warned us that the police would be showing up any minute.

We put Beatrice, along with all of our things, into a third vehicle, which was owned by the family whose house we were using. We weren't sure where to go, but we knew we had to leave. Beatrice's parents decided to go to the police and talk with them, to turn themselves in. In the meantime, we would try to get to a safe place to continue with our plan to deprogram Beatrice. Our thinking was that we could still have a successful deprogramming, thus making this whole situation with the police go away—like what happened in Ireland. The parents were desperate. They had come all the way from Sweden and wanted so much for this to work. It was obvious they loved their daughter more than anything and were worried they would never see her again if this failed.

It wasn't a very good plan to just take off like that, but it was made under a great deal of panic. I wasn't involved in the decision-making. It didn't occur to me until we were on the road that there were no family members with us, an essential ingredient to any deprogramming. There were hired security people, but that was different. Ideally, security people (who stand by exits and block them) aren't hired; they are friends and family members. But since Beatrice's family was from out of the country, this was their only option. She didn't know any of us and the security team had never met the deprogramming team.

My major challenge was always the notion that deprogrammers were vehicles of Satan (or whatever the particular cult's word was for evil). Family members were also considered to be influenced by Satan. Even so, the love of family members was hard to ignore as they sat in the deprogramming room or waited outside, bringing in food and listening to what was being said. Their concern during the days of discussion was always a crucial part of the client feeling safe. Also, the fear of being physically hurt was diminished with family members around. In Beatrice's situation, we would have none of those benefits.

All I knew about the plan was that we were going to take Beatrice to a cabin in the mountains. It was dark when we left the house, which we were happy about, but it was a long drive and the gas tank was nearly empty. We couldn't talk about the situation, but we were terrified Beatrice would start to scream when we pulled into a gas station. Fortunately, she was giving us the silent treatment and we left the gas station without event, breathing a collective sigh of relief. She didn't know anything that was going on at that point. We tried to talk with her as we would in a normal deprogramming, but a van was not very conducive to what we were trying to accomplish.

When we finally got to the cabin, we realized it would be a very difficult environment in which to work. There were no sheets, towels, or even adequate cooking supplies. And we had no food. Usually, those were things we didn't have to think about. Our only focus was supposed to be providing support and information for the cult victim.

Our responsibility was to create a psychological space for the cult member to look at and question her original decision to join. Once we accomplished the task of creating a safe psychological space, the next step would be to provide valid, logical information she could use to make a decision about her life going forward. If we were successful, that decision would be made without the chains of the cult's mental manipulation affecting her brain function. But in these conditions, we found we were nowhere near creating a safe psychological space. In fact, we were further from that than we had been when she arrived at the house initially.

Scott and I found ourselves at odds with the "security" guys who were suddenly sharing this adventure. No one was in charge, and we had never worked with these men before. They knew each other, and Scott and I knew each other. They were very concerned about risk, and about the fact that they hadn't been paid yet and might not get paid at all. We kept telling them that the only way out of this was to get Beatrice deprogrammed. They understood but had little patience. I was beginning to lose faith that we could get the job done, but agreed with Scott that we had to try.

One of the guys went to a convenience store and bought them out of potato salad, bread, cold cuts, chips and anything else that could be easily eaten without preparation. After a few days, we were able to get through to someone who could at least tell us what was going on. We were told we should get a different vehicle and leave the cabin—just in case. The police were definitely looking for us. The security guys kept talking about just letting her go and getting out of there. We still thought if we could only get to a decent place, we could finish our job. I could tell Scott was really concerned about Beatrice's parents and sincerely wanted the best for her and her family.

Someone I had never met, but who was a friend of the family who owned the cabin, brought us a different van and we headed out again. Beatrice was showing no signs of openness to what we had to say.

Through some of his connections, Scott finally found a place we could go. There was much debate about the decisions, which I tried to avoid. Ultimately, Scott took charge. We were going to Kansas.

It was an all-day drive and everyone was exhausted. Beatrice was argumentative. It was better than not talking to us, but we were clearly not where we wanted to be with her. We tried to take advantage of the driving time, but we had so many strikes against us that it was an uphill climb just to try to dig out of the psychological hole we were in with her, let alone being in a position to guide her out of the Moonies.

We finally pulled up to the address Scott had been given. When the van stopped and I woke from having dozed off, I hoped what I was seeing was part of my dream. This was the kind of town where everyone knows everyone's business and strangers turn heads. Scott asked me to go inside with him to meet the people who would be our hosts, sort of. They owned an antique/junk store on the main strip of town. It was one of half a dozen stores on Main Street. Above the store was an apartment they were getting ready to rent.

It had nothing in it. Nothing. Yet that was where we were going to do the deprogramming. Our "hosts" brought up some blankets and a couple of mattresses and chairs for us, not that it mattered to me—by then, I could have fallen asleep anywhere. The security guys decided to take turns staying awake. I went to sleep immediately.

The next thing I knew it was morning and someone was yelling "shit!" Beatrice was gone. She had somehow gotten out of the second story bathroom window. Scott and I grabbed our stuff and went downstairs. The others took off; I had no idea where they went. The guy who owned the shop was downstairs. He told us his pickup was in the alley. We went out the side door.

As soon as we got outside, we saw the truck and got in. As we looked up, we saw a police car go by the street in front of us. We got down so they couldn't see us. "The key," Scott said in frantic whisper.

"Shit!" I answered. We started looking around. I looked in the glove compartment and found nothing and then Scott found a key ring on the floor. He tried it. It fit the ignition.

We eased out of the alley, made a right onto the street and another right at the next corner. Another police car went speeding past as we were turning the corner. They were hurrying to the building we had just left. Within a few minutes we were on a country road heading out of town. We didn't care which direction at that point. A few miles down the road we realized we were almost out of gas. Fortunately, Scott discovered there was a lever that switched to an auxiliary gas tank. After driving for a few miles, Scott stopped at a phone booth and made a call. We drove to the house of someone he knew a couple of hours away. They bought us plane tickets and by the end of the day, I was back in Oregon.

Arrests were made shortly thereafter. Scott was one of the two people charged with kidnapping. Beatrice had identified him through her description. Scott had been outspoken as an advocate for anti-cult work much more than I had, and they were able to track him down with little effort. The other person arrested was a detective from Nebraska. The story made the news and my parents heard about the case. My mom called right away. She said she had a feeling I was involved. I told her that she was right, but that I was done deprogramming and had started looking for a job—the kind that had benefits and a steady paycheck, even if it wouldn't make me rich. I was hanging up my deprogramming shoes once and for all. I was twenty-seven years old. It had been a decade since I had joined the Moonies and I decided it was time to put it all behind me.

CHAPTER 28

I FOUGHT THE LAW
Bobby Fuller Four

I STARTED WORKING at Oregon Health Sciences University, a large hospital/medical school in Portland. My job was working the switchboards. Mostly I worked days, but sometimes filled in for people on the swing shift, 3:00 to 11:00 p.m., and on a rare occasion I would work graveyard, 11:00p.m. to 7:00a.m. During the day the job was fast paced, constantly answering and transferring call after call. The after-hours shifts dealt mostly with patients who were put on hold while we paged the doctor on call, who was covering that specialty.

I made casual friendships with the other switchboard operators. When there was a lull in the calls, we talked about everything from movies to relationships. Several of the people working there were going to school. Since OHSU was part of the Oregon State system of higher education, I had access to a great education benefit. Taking classes at any state school was nearly free. I discovered that this was how a lot of people got through college; they were working there specifically to get the benefit. I began to contemplate it myself.

Paula had started working on her master's degree and it seemed like too much to have both of us going to school at the same time, so I put that idea aside. I started settling into a lifestyle of working and doing home improvement projects, and enjoyed being part of a couple.

During a visit with my parents, my mom asked me if I was dating any men. I took a deep breath and said, "No, I don't date men," underlining the word men with my tone. My dad was sitting at the table nearby.

"You don't?" Mom asked in a whiny voice.

Dad piped in from across the room, annoyed by her line of questioning and the tone of her voice. "Honey, why do you act like we don't know this?" I turned to him feeling like there was an electric current running through my body. "You know Max was gay," he went on. Max was my uncle who had died in a car accident before I was born. I knew he had been very close to Dad.

The conversation changed to what felt like the first real conversation I had with my parents since I was a child. We talked about Paula and if I would ever have kids, and whether they needed to worry about AIDS. I explained to them that I did want to have kids and that lesbian couples did that, and that as far as AIDS went I was safer than if I were heterosexual.

That same year, Dad was rushed to the hospital in severe pain. Mom called to tell me he had been diagnosed with multiple myeloma, cancer of the bone marrow. She started to cry on the phone. So did I. I made several trips to Nebraska following his diagnosis and learned to know and love my family again.

It had been almost two years since the failed deprogramming in Colorado, and I had avoided the anti-cult world since then. One evening, though, there was a fundraiser going on for a local organization called the Positive Action Center that supported families with loved ones in cults. They had called and asked if I could come. I decided to do it, even though I was never very involved with the group. The couple that ran it was really nice, and I wanted to help if I could.

I ran into a guy I knew there, Garry, who had come with me on an attempted deprogramming in Canada, which ultimately never happened. We had a casual conversation. He knew Scott and we talked about the Colorado case. He asked me several questions.

There was something about him that gave me the creeps. I thought he was coming on to me, but there was something else that bothered me about him. I didn't know what. He was too clingy and didn't seem to pick up on subtle cues. When I tried to excuse myself to go talk with other people, he would ask me another question. I left early that evening because of him and decided I really was ready to leave that part of my life behind.

I was still seeing Andrea every week; the work I did with her kept me grounded. I was building an internal structure. What structure I had as a confused seventeen year old, before joining the group, had been dismantled and rebuilt by the Moonies around the doctrine that Moon was the Messiah, and that my only purpose in life was to serve him. That came crashing down during my deprogramming. Each week in her little office I would try to glue more pieces of myself together.

I transferred to a different department at OHSU and worked as a dispatcher for their public safety department. It was like being a dispatcher for 911, but scaled way down. I dispatched the officers to open doors for people who locked themselves out of their office or car. Sometimes there would be someone in the ER who needed to be transferred to the psych ward and the officers assisted with that, but it was fairly casual. It paid a little better than the switchboard, and was something different. I had been getting a little bored on the switchboard, so I enjoyed the change—until they put me on graveyard shift.

I tried everything to sleep better during the day: dark blinds to keep the light out, earplugs, and herbal sleeping pills, but I just couldn't get enough sleep.

After a few weeks of sleep deprivation, I realized I was really not doing well and was afraid I might have to quit. One morning, after I had finally gotten to sleep around 10:00 a.m., the doorbell rang. I tried to ignore it, but whoever it was kept knocking and ringing the bell. I finally went downstairs and opened the door.

"Are you Diane Benscoter?" a man in a suit asked me. There was another man next to him, similarly dressed.

"Yes," I answered.

He showed me his badge. "We're from the FBI," he said. "You are under arrest." He began reading me my rights. I invited them into the house where they told me I was a fugitive of the state of Colorado.

It took me a few minutes to realize they were there to take me with them. I was going to jail. "Can I change?" I asked. I was wearing pajamas. I explained that I worked graveyard shift and had been sleeping. One of them went upstairs with me and stood outside the door while I put on some clothes. I came out after getting dressed. "Can I call someone to tell them what's going on?" I asked. They looked at each other and the taller one said "Go ahead."

They were very nice to me. They had obviously been briefed about the "kidnapping" and were curious about it. They seemed almost sorry to have to arrest me. I tried to call Paula, but there was no answer. I tried one more number, but they were running out of patience. I called the cult awareness network number where I had volunteered at the fundraiser, and left a message asking for their help. I wrote a note on a white board in the kitchen. *I'm in jail. Please come get me out.*

We headed for the door. I hadn't noticed the car parked outside of my house with bars in the backseat. One of the agents took out a set of handcuffs. "Do I have to wear those?" I asked. I was worried about what my neighbors would think. They looked at each other and he put them away. We went to the car. He put his hand on my head and pushed down as I got into the backseat.

They asked me more questions as we drove downtown and entered the underground parking that led to the jail. The driver got out and came around the car. "Sorry," he said, "but we have to put these on you now." He put my arms behind my back and cuffed my wrists together. Inside, the two agents wished me good luck and left me there to be fingerprinted and to have my mug shots taken.

From that point on I might as well have been a bank robber. I was shocked at how the officials treated me. It didn't help that I was almost delirious from lack of sleep, but somehow everything seemed completely unreal.

There was someone getting fingerprinted in front of me. The woman taking his fingerprints looked disgusted, and I understood why. He looked like he belonged on the most-wanted list. When it was my turn I thought I would be treated better, more like the FBI agents had treated me, but she had the same look of disgust for me that she did for him.

After the mug shots, an officer escorted me to a holding cell. It was a small concrete room. There was a metal toilet and sink and a small metal bed attached to the wall, with a gross plastic pad on it. I stepped in and when I turned around the door was closing loudly. It had a sound of heavy permanence as it clamped shut. I had to go to the bathroom but there was no way I was going anywhere near that toilet; besides, anyone walking by could have seen me peeing. I sat on the bed and leaned against the wall. There was something on the wall next to me that looked like dried mustard. My eyes stung from lack of sleep, so I closed them. Tears began to form, but it seemed even my tears were reluctant to flow in that place. I just wanted to sleep. I wanted to ask for a blanket and pillow but there was no one to ask. I couldn't lie down there. I felt grossed out just leaning on the wall.

I dozed off sitting there. So many times I had fallen asleep sitting up in the Moonies, held captive by my invisible chains. There was a familiarity that made me claustrophobic. After what must have been a few hours, someone came and moved me to another cell. There was a phone in the cell, which seemed strange. It also seemed a lot cleaner. I picked up the receiver on the phone and there was a dial tone, so I called my house. Paula answered. She told me the people from the Positive Action Center were getting the money together to bail me out. She seemed frantic.

By late afternoon an officer came to my cell and unlocked the door. "This way," he said, like I was a dog. I followed him down the hall where I saw familiar faces. Anne, from the support group, was there, waiting to take me home. She and her husband had somehow put the bail money together to get me out.

I called work when I got home and told them what had happened and that I couldn't make it to work that night. The next day, I went to see a public defender.

Within a few days, I was offered a deal—a plea bargain.

Chapter 29

Return to Innocence
Enigma

M̲Y ATTORNEY STRONGLY ADVISED ME to take the plea bargain that was being offered. It was two years of unsupervised probation for a guilty plea. At the end of the two years, it would be expunged from my record. During those two years, if I was arrested and convicted of any felony, the kidnapping charges would be added onto any other conviction. I would definitely have to stop doing deprogramming.

That didn't bother me. I had already made that decision. Saying the word "guilty" was what bothered me.

Scott and the detective who snatched Beatrice off the street in Colorado were both arrested shortly after the failed deprogramming took place and had by this time gone to court over it. They ultimately prevailed with a "lesser evil" defense. The jury decided that although what took place was illegal, it was justified because it was done to protect Beatrice from a worse fate. It was explained to me that the lesser evil defense is rarely used, and even more rarely prevails.

If I did go to court, I would face a different jury and could easily be convicted and face prison time. Also, the cost of going to court in another state, and hiring a good attorney who understood deprogramming, would be tens of thousands of dollars, which I did not have.

When I talked with the people from the Positive Action Center, I discovered that I had not been identified, and most likely never would have been, until Garry—the guy at the fundraiser I attended—went to the police and told them about my involvement in the case. He gave them my name and told them how to find me.

The thought of fighting this seemed like more than I could handle. Dad's cancer had progressed; it had caused damage to his kidneys, and he was on dialysis. My stomach was starting to bother me again. Paula, my family, and my attorney all felt very strongly that I should take the plea bargain. So I did.

I would have to go to Colorado and go before a judge to enter my guilty plea. Mom, Dad and my sister Julie came to Colorado to be with me. We stayed at my uncle's house. Dad looked pretty good in spite of the treatment he was undergoing. I felt closer to the three of them than I had my entire life.

An attorney was there to represent me. He walked me through what would happen ahead of time. I would be asked some simple questions about my name and address, and then the judge would ask me how I pled to the charges, guilty or not guilty.

I went before the judge and it was exactly like the attorney had explained. "How do you plead?" the judge asked.

"Not guilty" I quickly said.

They all looked at each other. There were a few moments of silence before I realized what I had done. "Oh, I'm sorry. Sorry," I repeated. "I was supposed to say guilty." I felt like an idiot. I didn't feel guilty, but I hadn't changed my mind. It just came out wrong.

The judge spent some time making certain I understood what I was doing. "This is a serious charge," he said.

"I know, your Honor," I said. "Really, it just came out wrong." He did not seem amused, nor did the attorney representing me.

"Let's start over," the judge finally said, and asked me the questions again from the beginning.

This time, I said "Guilty." It felt very wrong coming out of my mouth, however.

That was the last time I had anything to do with the anti-cult world. The following year, Dad passed away. He never met my daughter, whom I adopted the year after he died. As I write this, she is a few months from the age I was when I first met the Moonies on my "Walk for World Peace."

Afterword

MORE THAN ONE of my friends during the writing of this book suggested that I watch a recently released documentary about Jonestown. When I finished the memoir, I rented the DVD and reluctantly hit play. Watching it made me physically ill; the film's images are now burned into my mind.

There was footage of a young man being interviewed, apparently by another member of the People's Temple, as Jonestown was first being built in the jungles of Guyana. He was one of the first to go to there, and his testimony of life in Jonestown was filled with the vision of an ideal in which he firmly believed. He couldn't have been more than 20 years old. His happiness and the light in his eyes glimmered as he proclaimed that he never wanted to leave Jonestown.

He made it out alive to tell his story and to be interviewed, 30 years later, for the documentary. I see myself in him—both the dedicated young man and the survivor, who is about my age.

There was a handwritten note shown and read at the end of the documentary, written by a member before he drank the poison that took his life. He asks in the note that what they were trying to do at Jonestown never be forgotten.

Then there is the image of the bodies, mostly lying face down, arms wrapped around each other: mother and baby, elderly, black and white. Over 900 people lying dead.

There were interviews with a handful of survivors. Several described holding a loved one as they died. One described details like the foam coming from the mouth of his young son. Another described laying the body of his wife next to her grandmother, as she had requested, as she was dying in his arms. Another talked tearfully of the death not only of her family members, but also of a dream that died that day.

I thought of how my own dream had died. I went back and looked again at the picture of 17-year-old me, standing with a sign in my hand proclaiming the One World Crusade and World Peace, and wondered what I would have done for my Messiah.

I felt a tragic kinship with extremists. I went online and put in the search term "suicide bomber." An image appeared in front of me of a leg, a woman's leg with a shoe still on the foot, but no body. At the knee, only flesh oozing. A chalk line was drawn around it. I have a pair of shoes that look like the one on her foot.

I know why she detonated. I know why a mother injected poison into her baby's mouth. They were not acts of hatred but of love, of deep belief.

I wonder how the people I deprogrammed are now. I am infinitely grateful that I am free from the circular logic that held me captive and created the possibility for unthinkable acts. I wonder if the people I helped deprogram also feel that way. I wonder if the trauma I was part of creating, as we intentionally yanked away their belief system, is a wound from which they have finally healed.

The human brain is an undiscovered frontier as vast as the universe in which we live. Advances are being made, however, and at unprecedented rates—gradually unraveling the mysteries of outer and inner space. I cannot pretend to be an expert on the brain, but I know something happened inside my brain that affected my decision-making processes, and I see similarities of varying degrees throughout the world.

Easy answers to hard questions were very appealing to me as a confused 17-year-old. Being part of community with a clear and well-defined idealistic goal was exhilarating. I feel certain Hitler Youth felt a similar psychological draw as they moved toward their totalistic indoctrination. I also know I share more with the woman whose leg was circled with chalk than just similar shoes.

As I look at pictures of Sun Myung Moon, I don't see an evil man. He believes he is God. His followers believe he is God. His doctrine, however, creates circular logic and a totalistic environment. Totalism creates an "us and them" mentality. As a dedicated member of the "us" of which I belonged, I know I would have drunk the Kool-Aid.

NOTES

1. According to the teachings, Sun Myung Moon was born without original sin, like Jesus, and in marrying his wife she became sinless. They became the True Parents of the world. Their children are considered to be born sinless and to be the first in a lineage of perfect people, embodiments of God. Hyo Jin was their first son. His wife, Nansook Hong, was chosen for him by Moon and the "perfect couple" had five children.

In 1995, Nansook left Hyo Jin and later published a book about her life with him. As she describes her life in the book, she experienced physical and mental abuse so extreme she eventually fled in the middle of the night with their children, after 14 years of marriage, fearing for her safety and that of her children. Her book, *In the Shadow of the Moons: My Life in the Reverend Sun Myung Moon's Family* describes the abuse she endured, including her husband's ongoing infidelity, cocaine addiction, and physical abuse as long as she could. She was beaten often. Hyo Jin told her that he got a thrill from violence. He threatened to punch her in the stomach when she was carrying his baby. After the divorce, Hyo Jin went to jail for refusing to pay her legal fees, and the Moon family had no more to do with their "perfect grandchildren." Hyo Jin was later re-married and had five more children. He died in 2008 of a heart attack. Allegations have also been brought that Moon's other son, Hyun Jin, has physically assaulted members of the church.

2. In Robert Lifton's book, *Thought Reform and the Psychology of Totalism*, he suggests a set of criteria against which any environment may be judged—a basis for answering the ever-recurring question: "Isn't this just like brainwashing?"

Lifton's criteria consist of eight, interdependent psychological themes. He states in his book: "In combination they create an atmosphere which can temporarily energize or exhilarate, but which at the same time poses the gravest of human threats." The psychological themes described in his book and listed below were each present and had a strong effect on my thought processes during my early months with the Unification Church. They were consistently present throughout my time with the group. They include:

MILIEU CONTROL

The most basic feature is the control of human communication within an environment.

If the control is extremely intense, it becomes internalized control—an attempt to manage an individual's inner communication.

Control over all a person sees, hears, reads and writes (information control) creates conflicts in respect to individual autonomy.

Groups express this in several ways: Group process, isolation from other people, psychological pressure, geographical distance or unavailable transportation, sometimes physical pressure.

Often a sequence of events, such as seminars, lectures, group encounters, which become increasingly intense and increasingly isolated, making it extremely difficult—both physically and psychologically—for one to leave.

Sets up a sense of antagonism with the outside world; it's "us against them."

Closely connected to the process of individual change (of personality).

MYSTICAL MANIPULATION (planned spontaneity)

Extensive personal manipulation.

Seeks to promote specific patterns of behavior and emotion in such a way that it appears to have arisen spontaneously from within the environment, while actually it has been orchestrated.

Totalist leaders claim to be agents chosen by God, history, or some supernatural force, to carry out the mystical imperative.

The "principles" (God-centered or otherwise) can be put forcibly and claimed exclusively, so that the cult and its beliefs become the only true path to salvation (or enlightenment).

The individual then develops the psychology of the pawn, and participates actively in the manipulation of others.

The leader who becomes the center of the mystical manipulation (or the person in whose name it is done) can be sometimes more real than an abstract god and therefore attractive to cult members.

Legitimizes the deception used to recruit new members and/or raise funds, and the deception used on the "outside world."

THE DEMAND FOR PURITY

The world becomes sharply divided into the pure and the impure, the absolutely good (the group/ideology) and the absolutely evil (everything outside the group).

One must continually change or conform to the group "norm."

Tendencies toward guilt and shame are used as emotional levers for the group's controlling and manipulative influences.

Once a person has experienced the totalist polarization of good/evil (black/white thinking), he has great difficulty in regaining a more balanced inner sensitivity to the complexities of human morality.

The radical separation of pure/impure is both within the environment (the group) and the individual.

Ties in with the process of confession—one must confess when one is not conforming.

CONFESSION

Cultic confession is carried beyond its ordinary religious, legal and therapeutic expressions to the point of becoming a cult in itself.

Sessions in which one confesses to one's sins are accompanied by patterns of criticism and self-criticism, generally transpiring within small groups with an active and dynamic thrust toward personal change.

Is an act of symbolic self-surrender.

Makes it virtually impossible to attain a reasonable balance between worth and humility.

A person confessing to various sins of pre-cultic existence can both believe in those sins and be covering over other ideas and feelings that s/he is either unaware of or reluctant to discuss.

Often a person will confess to lesser sins while holding on to other secrets (often criticisms/questions/doubts about the group/leaders that may cause them not to advance to a leadership position).

"The more I accuse myself, the more I have a right to judge you."

SACRED SCIENCE

The totalist milieu maintains an aura of sacredness around its basic doctrine or ideology, holding it as an ultimate moral vision for the ordering of human existence.

Questioning or criticizing those basic assumptions is prohibited.

A reverence is demanded for the ideology/doctrine, the originators of the ideology/doctrine, and the present bearers of the ideology/doctrine.

Offers considerable security to young people because it greatly simplifies the world and answers a contemporary need to combine a sacred set of dogmatic principles with a claim to a science embodying the truth about human behavior and human psychology.

LOADING THE LANGUAGE

The language of the totalist environment is characterized by the thought-terminating cliché (thought-stoppers).

Repetitiously centered on all-encompassing jargon.

"The language of non-thought."

Words are given new meanings—the outside world does not use the words or phrases in the same way—it becomes a "group" word or phrase.

DOCTRINE OVER PERSON

Every issue in one's life can be reduced to a single set of principles that have an inner coherence to the point that one can claim the experience of truth and feel it.

The pattern of doctrine over person occurs when there is a conflict between what one feels oneself experiencing and what the doctrine or ideology says one should experience.

If one questions the beliefs of the group or the leaders of the group, one is made to feel that there is something inherently wrong with them to even question; it is always "turned around" on them and the questioner/criticizer is questioned rather than the questions answered directly.

The underlying assumption is that doctrine/ideology is ultimately more valid, true and real than any aspect of actual human character or human experience and one must subject one's experience to that "truth."

The experience of contradiction can be immediately associated with guilt.

One is made to feel that doubts are reflections of one's own evil.

When doubt arises, conflicts become intense.

DISPENSING OF EXISTENCE

Since the group has an absolute or totalist vision of truth, those who are not in the group are bound up in evil, are not enlightened, are not saved, and do not have the right to exist.

"Being versus nothingness."

Impediments to legitimate being must be pushed away or destroyed.

One outside the group may always receive his or her right of existence by joining the group.

Fear manipulation—if one leaves this group, one leaves God or loses his/her transformation, or something bad will happen to him/her.

The group is the "elite," outsiders are "of the world," "evil," "unenlightened," etc.

Excerpted from: Thought Reform and the Psychology of Totalism
(Chapel Hill, 1989), Chapter 22, and The Future of Immortality *(New York 1987), Chapter 155*

3. Moon is famous for his mass marriages. These ceremonies are known as "The Blessing." These "blessings" are the only way God can rescue human beings from the satanic nature within them all. According to the doctrine, because sin occurred when Adam and Eve had sex prematurely (i.e., before God gave them permission), the Messiah's mission is to redeem that sin. The entire world will eventually be restored because sin will be abolished through pure children. Once the Messiah chooses a mate for one of his followers and they receive the blessing, they become a "blessed couple." Their children are then born free of the original sin.

We were taught that once anyone has heard the Divine Principle and has become aware of the root of sin and how it originally occurred, they are required to be celibate until Moon chooses their mate and they receive The Blessing. To commit the sin of being sexual after hearing the Divine Principle and before being "blessed" by Moon would be like knowingly spitting in God's face. It was made very clear that members could not receive The Blessing if they committed this *worst of all* sins. Any physical attraction was cause for great repentance. "Brothers" and "sisters" were separated as much as possible to prevent such attractions from forming.

4. According to the Divine Principle, the Messiah's key responsibility is to restore what happened in the Garden of Eden in which

Adam and Eve had sex before God blessed their union. This would happen through the sacred marriage with his current wife, the "True Mother."

Many allegations have been made that Moon had "cleansing" ceremonies with early female members of the church in which he had ritual sex with them. This was years before his marriage to his current wife. It is also alleged that he has a son from another woman in the organization, conceived during his marriage to his current wife and raised by one of his closest associates. These are just some of the many testimonies from ex-members, and even those still inside, which detail Moon's promiscuous sex life as well as his "perfect children's" similar infidelity.

Through all these obvious contradictions, members find ways to justify their belief in Moon and his doctrine of cleansing sin through the "Blessing." It is clear that rational thought cannot take place if these contradictions are to make sense. Yet intelligent men and women remain loyal to these teachings.

5. Sun Myung Moon's personal wealth and lavish lifestyle is well documented. Many articles and several books have documented his financial dealings, including tax fraud, for which he served time in prison. His political connections have also been well documented and tie him to the Bush family as well as numerous other high-profile politicians.

6. Flo Conway and Jeff Siegelman are well recognized for their book *Snapping—America's Epidemic of Sudden Personality Change*. It was first published in 1978 and looks closely at religious cults and the psychological phenomena in which the vulnerabilities of the human mind could be manipulated into "snapping" into sudden and drastic personality change. A second edition was published in 1995, further documenting their continuing research into these phenomena as well as expanding on the idea by placing their findings into a new category of disorder called "information disease," an alteration of a person's everyday information-processing capacities.

The earlier version of their book was widely used by deprogrammers to help the people to whom they were speaking. It was one of the books Elaine had with her when she came to talk with me.

It is the sudden personality change that alarms the family and friends of those who join cults and the reason this Underground Railroad, of sorts, grew. It was a desperate response to this "epidemic."

7. There are stories of deprogrammers using abusive methods and even sex as part of their technique. In my years of experience, I never came across anyone who used such techniques. From my exposure to the underground world of deprogramming, I would describe it as consisting mostly of people who had been directly affected by a cult—either they had been in a cult or a loved one had been or still was in a cult. They were sincere in their desire to help the families of those affected as well as the victim. They were also untrained and unregulated.

8. PTSD symptoms most commonly observed in ex-cult members are anxiety, depression, suicidal ideation, sleeplessness, violent outbursts, memory loss, vivid flashbacks and somataform disorder. "The sample from the Millon Clinical Multiaxial Inventory (MCMI-I) of ex-cultists can be characterized as having abnormal levels of distress in several of the personality and clinical symptoms scales. Research strongly suggests that the level of post-cult distress is quite high." (Martin, Langone, Dole, & Wiltrout, 1992, p. 219).

Taken from an independent research project by Ilona C. Cuddy

ABOUT THE AUTHOR

A T 17, DIANE BENSCOTER joined The Unification Church—the religious cult whose members are commonly known as "Moonies." After five long years, her distressed family arranged to have her deprogrammed. Benscoter then left The Unification Church, and was so affected by her experience that she became a deprogrammer herself. She devoted her time to extracting others from cults, until she was arrested for kidnapping. The shock of her arrest caused her to abandon her efforts for almost 20 years.

DIANE IS NOW DEDICATED to speaking out about extremism and how to lower vulnerability to what she defines "viral memetic infections." Her TED talk on the subject of how cults rewire the brain can be viewed at: www.ted.com/talks/ex_moonie_diane_benscoter_how_cults_think.html. Or check out Diane's website at www.DianeBenscoter.com

CPSIA information can be obtained at www.ICGtesting.com
Printed in the USA
LVOW12s1117300913

354733LV00003B/63/P

9 781939 051370